THE PRINCIPLES

OF THE

SOLUTION OF SENATE-HOUSE 'RIDERS'

EXEMPLIFIED BY THE SOLUTION OF THOSE PROPOSED IN THE EARLIER PARTS OF THE EXAMINATIONS OF THE YEARS 1848-1851.

BY

FRANCIS J. JAMESON, B.A.,

OF GONVILLE AND CAIUS COLLEGE, CAMBRIDGE.

Cambridge: MACMILLAN & Co.

London: GEORGE BELL; Dublin: HODGES & SMITH.

1851.

CAMBRIDGE:
PRINTED BY METCALFE AND PALMER.

CONTENTS.

INTRODUCTION.

THE Report of the Mathematical Board annually calls the attention of the Mathematical Students of this University to the importance of the Examples appended to the book-work questions in the Senate-House Examination Papers. The Board conceives that these Examples, or *Riders*, to use the more familiar term, afford a searching test of the merits of the candidates, and are peculiarly adapted to call forth an exhibition of *style*, which it must be allowed indicates the mathematician far more than a mere knowledge of books; and so high does it estimate their importance, that it has repeatedly recommended a diminution of the book-work questions in the Senate-House papers, in order to allow the admission of a larger number of Riders.

"To obtain," it observes, "a surer test of the acquaintance of the candidates with the subjects of their reading, examples and deductions have been attached to many of the propositions from books. The Board, however, having had before them an analysis of the answers to the questions proposed in 1846, 1847, 1848, and 1849, find that the number of answers to the examples and deductions has fallen below the amount which it is desirable to secure. They are of opinion that such a result may in a great measure be prevented by diminishing the number of questions, and they have agreed to recommend, that the papers containing the questions from books be shortened, in order to enable the candidates to give more time to Examples and Deductions."—*Report of Mathematical Board for* 1849.

The Report for 1850, with the same object in view, recommended a still further curtailment of the papers. The Report of the present year, while it again draws attention to the defect complained of in the former ones, acquaints us with the opinion of the Moderators aud Examiners, that the shortening of the papers has not had the desired effect. "It is obvious," it goes on to state, "that the only remedy lies in the previous practice and exercise of those who are to be examined," and in the students themselves "giving increased attention to the practical application of their reading. It is unnecessary to say anything in proof of the great importance of this portion of a mathematical examination, testing as it does very effectually the degree in which a student has really made himself master of the subjects which he professes to have read; and it is almost equally unnecessary to state, that a corresponding weight is attributed to it by the Moderators and Examiners, in estimating the relative merits of Candidates for Honours."

A few observations therefore on the principles of the solution of this class of questions, exemplified by the solution of those actually proposed in the Senate-House, will not, it is hoped, be altogether useless to those who may feel the want of direction in a branch of their studies which forms so essential a preparation for the Examination for Honours.

Riders we define to be original questions arising either directly or indirectly out of the propositions to which they are appended. For distinctness' sake, we may divide them into the three following classes :—

(1). The first and simplest kind are *direct examples* of a certain class of propositions; such, for instance, as investigate general rules for the various operations in different subjects. Examples of this kind are merely particular applications of the general rule which the proposition establishes, and must be answered by rigidly following out the method investigated in the foregoing book-work. It cannot be too carefully borne in mind by the student, that the value of his solution of an example of this class is in exact proportion to the *strictness* with which it corresponds with the proposition.

(2). Another kind consists of those questions in which some fact or property enunciated in a theorem immediately preceding has to be applied; *e. g.*

PROP. "If a quantity vary directly as (a) when (b) is invariable, and inversely as (b) when (a) is invariable, prove that it will vary as $\frac{a}{b}$, when both (a) and (b) are variable.

Ex. If 5 men and 7 boys can reap a field of corn of 125 acres in 15 days; in how many days will 10 men and 3 boys reap a field of corn of 75 acres, each boy's work being $\frac{1}{3}$ of a man's? (p. 24).

Under this head must be placed also all direct applications of *formulæ*. The point to be kept in mind is, that any solution independent of the formula or of the property enunciated in the proposition, however elegant in itself, and however excellent a solution of the question regarded as a *problem*, is altogether *valueless* as a solution of the *rider*.

(3). The third class consists of all those questions which are suggested by the proposition to which they are appended, or arise out of some particular part of the book-work investigation. This kind partakes more of the *problematical* character than the two former; but still we may in this case also apply the general observation, that the leading idea of the proposition or the method of its investigation should be the chief guide in the solution of the rider, and afford a pattern for its *style*.

It has been the aim of the following pages to follow out as closely as possible these principles. In all cases, the proposition has been given to which the question solved is a rider; and in several, a few observations have been made upon the proposition, which appeared necessary in order to connect it with the question appended. At the end of the book will be found a short collection of Examples for practice.*

We will conclude with a word of practical advice to the student. Let him not consider any proposition, or piece of book-work, to have been thoroughly mastered till he has diligently practised examples connected with it, so as to be able, when called upon in an Examination, to apply it readily to any required purpose. In this way his knowledge of mathematics will become sound and practical, and the science itself will become interesting and attractive. To commit to memory a number of theorems, and then to reproduce them in examination without the power of exemplifying their use, is a process no less dry than useless; but he who makes himself, in the true sense of the word, familiar with them by an intelligent observation of their different uses and applications, and by acquiring a readiness in illustrating their utility, receives the full benefit from the wise system according to which this University appoints mathematics as the basis of her training—requiring of her members to study this branch of science, not so much for the purpose of acquiring the knowledge of it, as of disciplining their own minds by *mastering* it.

---

* It will be perceived that no Examples are solved under the head of Astronomy; the reason being, that this subject, as treated in the earlier part of the Examination, consists almost entirely of popular explanations, and not of propositions which can be applied to Examples.

SOLUTIONS OF SENATE-HOUSE 'RIDERS.'

EUCLID.

1849. (*A*). Describe an equilateral triangle upon a given finite straight line. (*Euc.* I. 1.)

(*B*). By a method similar to that used in this problem, describe on a given finite straight line an isosceles triangle, the sides of which shall be each equal to twice the base.

Let AB (fig. 1) be the given finite straight line.

With centre A and radius equal to 2AB describe a circle CDF; and with centre B and radius equal to 2AB describe a circle CEF. Let the circles intersect in C. Join AC, BC. Then AC, BC being radii of the two circles are each equal to 2AB; and therefore ABC is the triangle required.

1850. (*A*). The opposite sides and angles of parallelograms are equal to one another; and the diameter bisects them. (*Euc.* I. 34.)

(*B*). If the opposite sides or the opposite angles of any quadrilateral figure be equal, or if its diagonals bisect one another, the quadrilateral is a parallelogram.*

1848. (*C*). If the two diameters be drawn, shew that a parallelogram will be divided into four equal parts.

---

* This question must be considered as belonging to the third class of 'Riders.' (See Introduction.)

Let ABCD be a quadrilateral. Join AC, BD (fig. 2).

1. Let AB = DC, and AD = BC. Since, then, in the two triangles ABD, CDB, two sides in one are equal to two sides in the other, each to each, and the third side BD is common to both, the triangles are equal, and therefore the angles, each to each.

$$\left.\begin{array}{r}\text{Therefore } \angle ABD = \angle CDB \\ \text{and } \angle ADB = \angle CBD\end{array}\right\} \text{ whence } \left\{\begin{array}{l} AB \parallel DC, \\ AD \parallel BC.\end{array}\right.$$

Hence ABCD is a parallelogram.

2. Let $\angle ABC = \angle ADC$, and $\angle BAD = \angle BCD$.

The three angles of triangle ABD = two right-angles = three angles of triangle CDB.

But $$\angle BAD = \angle BCD;$$

$$\therefore \angle ABD + \angle ADB = \angle BDC + \angle DBC.$$

Also $$\angle ABD + \angle DBC = \angle BDC + \angle ADB.$$

Adding these equals,

$$2\angle ABD + \angle ADB + \angle DBC = 2\angle BDC + \angle ADB + \angle DBC.$$

Taking away the common angles ADB, DBC, we get immediately

$$\angle ABD = \angle BDC,$$

whence also $$\angle DBC = \angle BDA.$$

Hence $$AB \parallel DC,$$

and $$AD \parallel BC.$$

And therefore ABCD is a parallelogram.

3. Let AE = EC and DE = EB.

Since also $$\angle AED = \angle CEB,$$

therefore the triangles ADE, CBE are equal, and

$$\angle ADE = \angle CBE;$$

whence $$AD \parallel BC.$$

Treating triangles AEB, CED in exactly the same manner as the triangles ADE, CBE, we obtain that

$$AB \parallel DC.$$

Hence ABCD is a parallelogram.

Solution of (*C*). By the latter part of (*A*) we have

$$\triangle ADC = \tfrac{1}{2}\,\text{parallelogram},$$
$$= \triangle DAB.$$

But the triangle AED is common; therefore

$$\triangle DEC = \triangle BEA.$$

By exactly similar reasoning,

$$\triangle AED = \triangle CEB.$$

Again, in the triangles AEB, CED, two angles are equal and AB = DC, therefore

$$EB = ED.$$

Therefore the triangles BCE, ECD, being upon equal bases and between the same parallels,* are equal to one another.

Hence $\triangle ECD = \triangle BCE = \triangle BEA = \triangle AED.$

1851. (*A*). Triangles upon equal bases and between the same parallels are equal to one another. (I. 38.)

(*B*). Let ABC, ABD be two equal triangles upon the same base AB, and on opposite sides of it: join CD meeting AB in E; shew that CE is equal to ED.

Make $\angle ABD' = \angle ABD$ and $BD' = BD$ (fig. 3). Join CD′, AD′, ED′. By construction,

$$\triangle ABD' = \triangle ABD,$$
$$= \triangle ABC, \text{ by hypothesis.}$$

By applying the proposition as in *Euclid* I. 39 and 40, we obtain that $D'C \parallel AB$.

Hence, because triangles CEB, D′EB are on the same base and between the same parallels,

$$\triangle CEB = \triangle D'EB,$$
$$= \triangle DEB, \text{ by the construction of the figure.}$$

Now the triangles CEB, DEB being equal and between the same parallels, must be on equal bases. For if not, let CE=EF.

---

* See Note, p. 5.

Then triangles CEB, FEB, being on equal bases and between the same parallels, are by (*A*) equal to one another. Hence $\triangle$FEB = $\triangle$DEB; that is, the less equals the greater, which is absurd. Therefore CE = ED.

1851. (*A*). In any right-angled triangle, the square described upon the side subtending the right angle is equal to the squares described on the sides which contain the right angle. (I. 47.)

(*B*). If ABC be a triangle whose angle A is a right angle, and BE, CF be drawn bisecting the opposite sides respectively; shew that four times the sum of the squares of BE and CF is equal to five times the square of BC.

$$4BE^2 = 4(AB^2 + AE^2) \text{ by } (A) \text{ (fig. 4)},$$
$$4CF^2 = 4(AC^2 + AF^2);$$
$$\therefore 4(BE^2 + CF^2) = 4(AB^2 + AC^2) + 4AE^2 + 4AF^2,$$
$$= 4BC^2 + AB^2 + AC^2,$$
$$= 4BC^2 + BC^2,$$
$$= 5BC^2.$$

1849. (*A*). Divide a given straight line into two parts, so that the rectangle contained by the whole and one of the parts shall be equal to the square of the other part. (II. 11.)

(*B*). Shew that in Euclid's figure, four other lines, beside the given line, are divided in the required manner.

It is at once manifest that CD (fig. 5) is divided in the required manner in K.

Also in the investigation of (*A*) it is shewn that

$$CF.FA = AB^2 = AC^2.$$

Thus CF is so divided in A, as is also therefore KG in the point H.

Moreover, since the triangles BHL, BAE, are similar, BE, BA are divided, similarly in the points L, K.*

Hence the lines CF, KG, CD, EB are divided in the same manner as the line AB.

1850. (*A*). Describe a square which shall be equal to a given rectangle. (II. 14.)

(*B*). Given a square, and one side of a rectangle which is equal to the square; find the other side.

If, in (*A*), AC (fig. 6) be the given rectangle, the proof of the proposition involves this construction. Produce AB to D, making BD = BC. On AD describe semi-circle AHD. Produce CB to H. It is then proved that

square on BH = rectangle AC.

We thus have suggested the following solution of (*B*):

Let AB be the given side of the rectangle: draw BH at right angles to AB, equal to a side of the given square. Join AH; make ∠AHE = ∠EAH; and with centre E and radius EA or EH describe the circle AHD. Then,

∵ AD is bisected in E,

rect. of AB, BD + sq. on EB = sq. on ED

= sq. on EH

= sq. on EB + sq. on BH,

and ∴ rect. of AB, BD = sq. on BH,

i. e. = given square.

Hence BD is the other side required.

1848. (*A*). Equal straight lines in a circle are equally distant from the centre; and, conversely, those which are equally distant from the centre are equal to one another. (III. 14.)

(*B*). Shew that all equal straight lines in a circle will be touched by another circle.

---

* In cases like the above it is not unallowable to assume the result of a well-known property, which in *Euclid* is proved subsequent to the proposition under consideration.

The proposition tells us that the perpendiculars from the centre of a circle on all equal straight lines in the circle are equal to one another. Therefore a circle may be described through the extremities of all these perpendiculars, having its centre at the centre of the given circle: and since each of the equal straight lines is thus drawn through the extremity of a diameter at right angles to it, each will be a tangent to the second circle.

1848. (*A*). The angle at the centre of a circle is double of the angle at the circumference upon the same base; that is, upon the same part of the circumference. (III. 20.)

(*B*). If two straight lines AEB, CED, in a circle, intersect in E, the angles subtended by AC and BD at the centre are together double of the angle AEC.

Join BC (fig. 7).

Then, angle subtended by AC at the centre

$$= \angle AOC,$$
$$= 2\angle ABC, \text{ by } (A).$$

The angle subtended by BD at the centre

$$= \angle BOD,$$
$$= 2\angle BCD.$$

Therefore $\angle AOC + \angle BOD = 2\angle EBC + 2\angle ECB,$

$$= 2\angle AEC.$$

1851. (*A*). The opposite angles of any quadrilateral figure inscribed in a circle are together equal to two right angles. (III. 22.)

(*B*). If a polygon of an even number of sides be inscribed in a circle, the sum of the alternate angles, together with two right angles, is equal to as many right angles as the figure has sides.

If the polygon is a quadrilateral, we have immediately from (*A*),

sum of alternate angles + 2 right angles = 4 right angles.

If the polygon have six or more sides, from any angular point A draw lines A_1A_4, A_1A_8 (fig. 8) to the *third* angular point on each side of A_1, cutting off *quadrilaterals*.* Since the number of remaining sides between A_4, A_8 is even, a certain number of quadrilaterals may be formed by joining every second angular point from A_4 with A_1.

All these quadrilaterals are inscribed in the circle; hence, by the proposition,

$$\angle A_1A_2A_3 + \angle A_3A_4A_1 = 2 \text{ right angles},$$

$$\angle A_1A_4A_5 + \angle A_5A_6A_1 = 2 \text{ right angles},$$

$$\angle A_1A_6A_7 + \angle A_7A_8A_1 = 2 \text{ right angles},$$

$$\angle A_1A_8A_9 + \angle A_9A_{10}A_1 = 2 \text{ right angles}.$$

Adding,

sum of alternate angles A_2, A_4, A_6, &c. = twice as many right angles as there are quadrilaterals

$$= 2\,(r-1) \text{ right angles},$$

if $2r$ is the number of sides of the polygon;

$\therefore$ sum of alternate angles + 2 right angles = $2r$ right angles
= as many right angles as there are sides.

1850. (*A*). In a circle, the angle in a semicircle is a right angle. (III. 31.)

(*B*). The greatest rectangle that can be inscribed in a circle is a square.

Here (*B*) is a direct application of the fact asserted in (*A*).

Let ABCD (fig. 9) be any rectangle inscribed in a circle. Join AC. By the proposition, $\because$ $\angle$ABC is a right angle, ABC is a semicircle.

Draw BE perpendicular to AC, and take F the centre.

---

* If the polygon has six sides, the lines A_1A_4, A_1A_8, will coincide.

Then rectangle ABCD = 2 triangle ABC
= rectangle on base AC, and between same parallels as the triangle ABC
= AC.BE.

Now AC, being the diameter of the circle, is constant; therefore the area of the rectangle is proportional to BE, and is greatest when BE is greatest, *i. e.* when it coincides with GF.

Hence the greatest rectangle inscribed in the circle is AGCH, which is evidently a square.

1850. (*A*). Cut off a segment from a given circle which shall contain an angle equal to a given rectilineal angle.

(*B*). Divide a circle into two segments, such that the angle in one of them shall be five times the angle in the other.

We may consider (*A*) as a direct application of the proposition that, "if from a point in a circle two lines be drawn, one touching and the other cutting the circle, the angle between them is equal to the angle in the alternate segment of the circle." (*B*) may be regarded as a direct application of the *same* proposition to a slightly different problem.

Draw AB touching the circle (fig. 10). Take any point B in the tangent; and on AB describe an equilateral triangle ABC. Bisect the angle BAC by the line AD.

Then $\angle DAB = \frac{1}{2} \angle CAB.$

But $\angle CAB = \frac{1}{3}$ of 2 right angles;

$\therefore \angle DAB = \frac{1}{6}$ of 2 right angles;

$\therefore \angle DAG = \frac{5}{6}$ of 2 right angles:

whence $\angle DAG = 5 \angle DAB.$

But $\angle DAG = \angle$ in segment AFD,

and $\angle DAB = \angle$ in segment AED;

$\therefore \angle$ in segment AFD = $5 \angle$ in segment AED.

Hence the circle is divided as required by the line AD.

1851. (*A*). Inscribe an equilateral and equiangular quindecagon in a given circle. (IV. 16.)

(*B*). In a given circle inscribe a triangle, whose angles are as the numbers 2, 5, and 8.

Let $A_1A_2 \ldots A_{15}$ be an equilateral and equiangular quindecagon inscribed in the given circle. Draw the lines A_1A_3, A_3A_8, A_8A_1, cutting off arcs which are to one another as 2, 5, 8. The angles $A_1A_8A_3$, $A_3A_1A_8$, $A_8A_3A_1$, which stand upon these arcs, will also be in this ratio; and therefore $A_1A_3A_8$ will be the triangle required.

1850. (*A*). Describe an isosceles triangle, having each of the angles at the base double of the third angle. (IV. 10.)

(*B*). Shew that the base of the triangle is equal to the side of a regular pentagon inscribed in the smaller circle of the figure.

In the investigation of (*A*) it is shewn that BD = DC (fig. 11).

If O is the centre of the small circle,

$$\angle COD = 2\,\angle CAD.$$

But by (*A*), the angles ABD, ADB are each double of BAD; therefore the sum of these 3 angles, or 2 right angles,

$$= 5\,\angle BAD;$$

$$\therefore\ \angle BAD = \tfrac{1}{5}\,(2 \text{ right angles}),$$

and

$$\angle COD = 2\,\angle BAD$$

$$= \tfrac{1}{5}\,(4 \text{ right angles}).$$

Hence CD, to which BD is equal, is the side of a regular pentagon inscribed in the circle ACD.

1851. (*A*). If the angle of a triangle be divided into two equal angles by a straight line, which also cuts the base, the segments of the base have the same ratio which the other sides of the triangle have to one another. (VI. 3.)

(*B*). If A, B, C, be three points in a straight line, and D a point at which AB and BC subtend equal angles, shew that the locus of the point D is a circle.

Produce AB to a point O, such that OB = OD* (fig. 12).

Then $\angle ODB = \angle OBD$

$= \angle OAD + \angle ADB$

$= \angle OAD + \angle CDB$;

$\therefore \angle ODC = \angle OAD$.

Also the angle AOD is common to the two triangles OCD, ODA. Hence these triangles are similar;

$\therefore$ OD : OC :: AD : DC :: AB : BC by the proposition;

or, since OD = OB,

OB : OC :: AB : BC;

which shews that O is a fixed point.

Hence the locus of D is a circle whose centre is O.

1849. (*A*). The sides about the equal angles of equiangular triangles are proportionals, and those sides which are opposite to the equal angles are homologous. (VI. 4.)

(*B*). Apply this proposition to prove that the rectangle contained by the segments of any chord passing through a given point within a circle is constant.

Let AB, CD (fig. 13) be any two chords of a circle intersecting in O. Join BC, AD.

Since the angles in the same segment of a circle are equal,

$\angle ABC = \angle ADC$, and $\angle BCD = \angle BAD$.

Hence the triangles BOC, DOA are equiangular. Therefore by (*A*), AO : DO :: OC : OB.

Therefore rect. of AO, OB = rect. of DO, OC.

---

* From the middle point of *BD* draw a line at right angles to it, cutting *AB* produced in *O*.

1850. (*A*). Find a third proportional to two given straight lines. (VI. 11.)

(*B*). AB is a diameter, and P any point in the circumference of a circle; AP and BP are joined and produced if necessary: if from any point C of AB a perpendicular be drawn to AB, meeting AP and BP in points D and E respectively, and the circumference of the circle in a point F, shew that CD is a third proportional to CE and CF.*

Draw PM perpendicular to AB, (fig. 14). From similar triangles CEB, MPB,

$$CE : MP :: CB : MB;$$

and from similar triangles CDA, MPA,

$$CD : MP :: AC : AM.$$

Compounding these ratios,

$$CE.CD : MP^2 :: AC.CB : AM.MB.$$

But $AM.MB = MP^2$, (III. 35);

$$\therefore CE.CD = AC.CB$$

$$= CF^2,$$

or $CE : CF :: CF : CD.$

1851. (*A*). If two straight lines be parallel, and one of them be at right angles to a plane, the other is at right angles to the same plane. (XI. 8.)

(*B*). From a point E draw EC, ED perpendicular to two planes CAB, DAB, which intersect in AB, and from D draw DF perpendicular to the plane CAB, meeting it in F; shew that the line joining the points C and F, produced if necessary, is perpendicular to AB.

Since EC, DF are perpendicular to the same plane, they are parallel (XI. 6), and therefore the points E, C, D, F, lie in one plane.

* This can only be considered as one of the third class of riders.

Let CF, or CF produced, meet AB in G. Draw GH parallel to EC or DF. Then, by (*A*), GH is at right angles to the plane CAB; and therefore ∠AGH is a right angle. Similarly, a line GH′ drawn parallel to ED will lie in the plane of ECD, and will be at right angles to the plane DAB. Therefore ∠AGH′ is a right angle. Hence AB will be at right angles to the plane in which GH, GH′ lie, (XI. 4), and therefore at right angles with the line CFG, which also lies in that plane.

1849. (*A*). Draw a straight line perpendicular to a plane from a given point without it. (XI. 11.)

(*B*). Prove that equal right lines drawn from a given point to a given plane are equally inclined to the plane.

Let P be the given point; PA, PA′, two equal straight lines drawn from P to meet the plane. As in (*A*) draw a perpendicular PN to the plane. Join NA, NA′.

By the definition of a perpendicular to a plane, PN makes right angles with every line in the plane drawn from N, and therefore with NA, NA′. Hence in the right-angled triangles PAN, PA′N, PA = PA′, and PN is common;

therefore NA = NA′, (I. 47),

and the triangles are equal.

Hence ∠PAN = ∠PA′N,

or the lines PA, PA′ are equally inclined to the plane.

GEOMETRICAL CONIC SECTIONS.

1848. (A). Assuming the tangent at any point P of a parabola to make equal angles with the focal distance SP and the diameter at that point, prove that SY, the perpendicular upon it from the focus, meets it in the tangent at the vertex.

(B). If PM be the ordinate at P, and T the intersection of the tangent at P with the axis, $TP.TY = TM.TS$.

Since, by (A), SYT (fig. 15) is a right angle, the triangles STY, PTM are similar.

Hence $TY : TS :: TM : TP$,

therefore $TP.TY = TM.TS$.

Or thus:

Since SYP, SMP are right angles, a circle can be described about $SYPM$. Therefore

$$TP.TY = TM.TS.$$

1851. (A). Assuming that the sum of the focal distances of a point in the ellipse is equal to a given line, shew that the axis-major is equal to the same line.

(B). Shew that the axis-major is greater than any other diameter.

Let PCP' (fig. 16) be any diameter. Join P and P' with the foci.

Then, since two sides of a triangle are greater than the third,

$$SP + SP' > PP',$$

and

$$HP + HP' > PP';$$

$$\therefore SP + HP + SP' + HP' > 2PP'.$$

But, by (A), $$SP + HP = SP' + HP'$$ $$= AA'.$$

Therefore $$2AA' > 2PP',$$

and therefore $$AA' > PP'.$$

1848. (A). If one of the focal distances SP of a point P be produced to L, a straight line PT which bisects the exterior angle HPL is the tangent to the curve at P.

(B). For what position of P is the angle SPH greatest?

By (A), (fig. 17),

$$\angle SPH + 2\angle SPT = 2 \text{ right angles.}$$

Therefore $\angle SPH$ is greatest when $\angle SPT$ is least.

Now as P moves from A to B, $\angle SPT$ decreases from a right angle to SBt (where $Bt \parallel CT$); and as P moves from B to A', $\angle SPT$ increases from SBt to a right angle.

Thus $\angle SPT$ is least, and therefore $\angle SPH$ is greatest, when P is at B.

1851. (A). In the ellipse if PU be a tangent at P, meeting the minor axis produced in U, and PN be drawn perpendicular to the minor axis, then

$$CN : CB :: CB : CU.$$

(B). If a series of ellipses be described having the same major axis, the tangents at the extremities of their latera-recta will all meet the minor axis in the same point.

Let SL (fig. 18) be the semi-latus-rectum of one of the ellipses, U the point where the tangent at L meets the minor axis. By (A),

$$CU : CB :: CB : SL.$$

But $$CB : SL :: CA : CB;$$

therefore $$CU : CB :: CA : CB,$$

and therefore $$CU = CA,$$

which is constant, since all the ellipses have the same major axis.

1850. (*A*). The perpendiculars from the foci on the tangent of an ellipse intersect the tangent in the circumference of a circle having the axis-major as diameter.

(*B*.) Employ this proposition to find the locus of the intersection of a pair of tangents at right angles to each other.

1849. (*C*). Deduce from the proposition an analogous one for the parabola.

(*B*). Let SY, HZ (fig. 19) be the perpendiculars from the foci on the tangents; Y, Z being by (*A*) points in circumference of the circle whose diameter is AA'.

If we produce YC to Z_1, and join HZ_1, we obtain from the triangles CSY, CHZ_1 that $HZ_1 = SY$, that HZ_1 is in the same straight line with ZH, and therefore that

$$SY.HZ = Z_1H.HZ = A'H.HA = BC^2.$$

Let the tangent at P meet the tangent which is at right angles to it in Q, which latter tangent suppose intersects the circle in Y', Z'. Join SY', HZ'.

By (*A*), SY', HZ' are perpendicular to QZ'; and therefore

$$QY' = SY, \quad QZ' = HZ.$$

Hence, drawing QKK' through the centre C,

$$\begin{aligned} QK.QK' &= QY'.QZ' \\ &= SY.HZ \\ &= BC^2. \end{aligned}$$

Therefore the distance of Q from C is constant, and the locus of Q is a circle whose centre is C.

(*C*). The ellipse will become a parabola if C moves off to an infinite distance, while the vertex A' and the focus H remain fixed. For, if C and therefore S move off to an infinite distance, PS will become parallel to $A'A$. Hence the tangent ZPY, which always makes equal angles with HP and PS, will in this case make equal angles with HP and a line through P parallel to $A'A$; and the curve will therefore be a parabola.

Now the locus of Z in the ellipse is a circle whose diameter is $A'A$; and when C moves off to an infinite distance, the radius of this circle becomes infinite, and the circle coincides with its tangent at the point A'.

Consequently, in the parabola, the locus of the intersection of the tangent with the perpendicular upon it from the focus is the tangent at the vertex.

1848. (*A*). In an ellipse the sum of the squares of any two conjugate diameters is invariable.

(*B*). When is the square of their sum least?

$$(CP + CD)^2 = CP^2 + CD^2 + 2\,CP.CD, \text{ (fig. 20)}$$
$$= AC^2 + BC^2 + 2\,CP.CD, \text{ by } (A).$$

Therefore $(CP + CD)^2$ will be least when $CP.CD$ is least.

But $$CD.PF = AC.BC;$$

$$\therefore\ CP.CD = AC.BC\,.\,\frac{CP}{PF},$$

therefore $CP.CD$ is least when $\frac{CP}{PF}$ is least; *i.e.* when $PF = CP$, or when CP, CD are at right angles. Hence $(CP + CD)^2$ is least when CP, CD coincide with CA, CB.

1848. (*A*). Prove that all parallelograms whose sides touch an ellipse at the ends of conjugate diameters are equal.

(*B*). Prove that such parallelograms have the least area of all which circumscribe the ellipse.

Let $T_1T_2T_3T_4$ (fig. 21) be a parallelogram circumscribing an ellipse at the extremities of conjugate diameters CP, CD; $t_1t_2t_3t_4$ another parallelogram circumscribing the ellipse.

Draw PF perpendicular to DCD'.

Then area of $T_1T_2T_3T_4 = 2PF.DD'$,

area of $t_1t_2t_3t_4 = 2PF.dd'$.

Now DD' is the least possible value of dd'; therefore area of $t_1t_2t_3t_4$ is always greater than that of $T_1T_2T_3T_4$.

But by (*A*), in whatever position the conjugate diameters CP, CD are drawn, the area $T_1T_2T_3T_4$ is constant. Consequently of the areas of all parallelograms circumscribing the ellipse, this constant area is the least.

1850. (*A*). In the hyperbola the rectangle under the lines intercepted between the centre and the intersections of the axis with the ordinate and tangent respectively, is equal to the square of the semi-axis major.

$$(CN.CT = AC^2).$$

(*B*). Through N draw NQ, parallel to AP, to meet CP in Q; prove that AQ is parallel to the tangent at P.

Since $$CN.CT = AC^2, \text{ (fig. 22)};$$

$$\therefore\ AC : CN :: CT : AC.$$

Now, since NQ is parallel to AP,

$$CP : CQ :: CA : CN,$$

$$:: CT : CA;$$

therefore AQ is parallel to TP.

1849. (*A*). Prove that the area of the triangle contained by the tangent and the asymptotes is constant.

(*B*). If SVs, TVt be two tangents cutting one asymptote in the points S, T, and the other in s, t; prove that

$$VS : Vs :: Vt : VT.$$

The proposition gives us

$$\triangle SCs = \triangle TCt, \quad \text{(fig. 23)}.$$

Take away the common part $SCTV$;

therefore $$\triangle SVT = \triangle tVS,$$

and $$\angle TVS = \angle SVt;$$

therefore, by *Euc.* VI. 15,

$$VS : Vs :: Vt : VT.$$

1849. (A). The section of a right cone by a plane parallel to a line in its surface, and perpendicular to the plane containing that line and the axis, is a parabola.

(B). The foci of all parabolic sections which can be cut from a given right cone lie upon the surface of another cone.

In the investigation of (A) we obtain

$$PN^2 = \frac{AL^2}{BL} \cdot AN. \quad \text{(fig. 24)}.$$

See Goodwin's *Course*, *Conics*, *Parabola*, prop. X.

This shews that the latus-rectum of the parabolic section

$$4AS = \frac{AL^2}{BL},$$

$$= \frac{AL^2}{BL^2} \cdot AB,$$

$$= \frac{CD^2}{BC^2} \cdot AB.$$

This proves that for all sections parallel to MAP, AS is proportional to AB; and therefore BS must be a fixed line.

Similarly, the foci of all sections parallel to other lines in the surface of the cone beside BC lie in lines through B inclined at a constant angle to the axis of the cone. Therefore all these foci lie on the surface of a cone.

1851. (A). If a right cone be cut by a plane which meets the cone on both sides of the vertex, the section is a hyperbola.

(B). Shew how to cut from a given cone a hyperbola whose asymptotes shall contain the greatest possible angle.

In the investigation of (A), in order to shew that the section PAR (fig. 25) is an hyperbola, we prove that

$$AN.NM : PN^2 :: BF^2 : FH^2,$$

which is the property of an hyperbola, the major axis of which is AM, and the minor axis is to AM as $FH : BF$. (Goodwin's *Course*, *Conic Sections*, *Hyperbola*, prop. xii.)

Hence the ratio $FH : BF$ is the tangent of the semi-angle between the asymptotes.* But the same ratio is the tangent of the angle FBH.

Therefore the angle between the asymptotes $= \angle GBH$.

Now $\angle GBH$ is greatest when it equals the vertical angle of the cone; that is, when BF is perpendicular to DE.

Hence the angle between the asymptotes will be greatest when the cutting plane PAR is parallel to the axis of the cone, and that angle will be equal to the vertical angle of the cone.

1851. (A). In the parabola, at any point P, the chord of curvature parallel to the axis and that through the focus are severally equal to $4SP$.

(B). If the circle of curvature at the point P intersect the parabola in another point R, and RQ, drawn parallel to the axis, meet the circle in Q, shew that PQ is the chord of curvature through the focus.

Draw PT (fig. 26), the tangent to the parabola or the circle of curvature, meeting RQ produced in T. Then

$$TQ.TR = TP^2 \text{ by property of the circle,}$$

$$TP^2 = 4SP.TR \text{ by property of the parabola.}$$

$$\therefore \ TQ.TR = 4SP.TR,$$

$$\therefore \ TQ = 4SP.$$

From this it follows that $PQ = TQ$. For if not, make $\angle TPQ' = \angle QTP$. Then PQ' will pass through the focus, and by (A) its length will $= 4SP = TQ$.

---

* See Goodwin, as above, prop. VII., where it is proved that the asymptotes are the diagonals of a rectangle whose sides are the major and minor axes.

But $$PQ' = T'Q',$$
therefore $$T'Q' = TQ,$$
which is impossible unless Q' coincide with Q.

Hence $$PQ = QT,$$
$$\therefore \angle QPT = \angle QTP,$$
which shews that PQ passes through the focus.*

1850. (A). Find the diameter of curvature at any point of an ellipse.

(B). If an ellipse, a parabola, and a hyperbola have a common tangent and the same curvature at the vertex, the ellipse will lie entirely within the parabola, and the parabola entirely within the hyperbola.

In the ellipse, diameter of curvature at $P = 2\dfrac{CD^2}{PF}$.

Hence .... at $A = 2\dfrac{BC^2}{AC}$.

Let S (fig. 27) be the focus of the parabola, ACM, BC the major and minor axes of the ellipse; $AC'M'$, $B'C'$ similar lines for the hyperbola.

Now, diameter of curvature at A in parabola $= 4AS$,

and .... hyperbola $= 2\dfrac{B'C'^2}{AC'}$;

and by hypothesis, $4AS = 2\dfrac{BC^2}{AC} = 2\dfrac{B'C'^2}{AC'}$.

In the parabola we have, if $NP'PP''$ be a common ordinate,
$$PN^2 = 4AS.AN;$$
in the ellipse, $$P'N^2 = \frac{BC^2}{AC^2}.AN.NM$$
$$= \frac{2AS}{AC}.AN.NM;$$

* The Author is indebted for this solution to the kindness of Mr. Gaskin.

in the hyperbola, $P''N^2 = \dfrac{B'C'^2}{AC'^2}.AN.NM'$

$$= \frac{2AS}{AC'}.AN.NM'.$$

But, since $2AC > NM$,

$$\therefore \frac{2AS}{AC}.AN.NM < 4AS.AN,$$

or $P'N < PN.$

And since $2AC' < NM'$,

$$\therefore \frac{2AS}{AC'}.AN.NM' > 4AS.AN,$$

or $P''N > PN.$

Hence the ellipse lies wholly within the parabola, and the parabola wholly within the hyperbola.

ALGEBRA.

1851. (*A*). Prove the rule for finding the greatest common measure of two quantities.

(*B*). Shew that the greatest common measure of the two numbers is equal to the greatest common measure of any divisor made use of in the process and the corresponding dividend.

Let the usual process for finding G.C.M. of a and b, be pursued, $C_1, C_2, C_3, \ldots$ being the successive remainders, $p_1, p_2, p_3, \ldots$ the successive quotients. One step in the process will be

$$\begin{array}{l} C_r \,)\; C_{r-1} \;(p_{r+1} \\ \quad\;\; \underline{p_{r+1} C_r} \\ \qquad\; C_{r+1} \end{array}$$

$$\therefore\; C_{r-1} - p_{r+1} C_r = C_{r+1}, \text{ and } C_{r-1} = p_{r+1} C_r + C_{r+1},$$

from which it follows that C_{r+1} contains the whole system of factors common to C_{r-1} and C_r, and that C_{r-1} contains all those common to C_r and C_{r+1}.

Hence, G.C.M. of

$$\begin{aligned} C_r \text{ and } C_{r+1} &= \text{G.C.M. of } C_{r-1} \text{ and } C_r \\ &= \text{(by the same reasoning), G.C.M. of } C_{r-2} \text{ and } C_{r-1} \\ &= \text{G.C.M. of } C_{r-3} \text{ and } C_{r-2}, \\ &\quad \&\text{c.} \\ &= \text{G.C.M. of } a \text{ and } b. \end{aligned}$$

1850. (*A*). Shew how to find the least whole number which is accurately divisible by each of two given whole numbers.

(*B*). Find the least number of ounces of standard gold that can be coined into an exact number of half-sovereigns; standard gold being coined at the rate of £3 17*s*. $10\frac{1}{2}d$. to an ounce.

In (*A*), if a, b be the two given numbers, d their greatest common divisor, the number required, *i.e.* their least common multiple, $= \dfrac{ab}{d}$.

In (*B*), if we find the number of shillings in the value of an ounce of gold and in half-a-sovereign, the least common multiple of these numbers divided by the number of shillings in the value of an ounce will give the least number of ounces that can be coined into an exact number of half-sovereigns.

Now £3 17*s*. $10\frac{1}{2}d. = 77s.\ 10\frac{1}{2}d. = 77s.\ 10{\cdot}5d.$

$$= 77\,\frac{10{\cdot}5}{12}s. = 77{\cdot}875s.,$$

and we have to find the least common multiple of 10 and 77·875.

By (*A*), the least common multiple of 10000 and 77875 is

$$\frac{10000 \times 77875}{\text{their G. C. M.}}.$$

But $$10000 = 2^4.5^4,$$

and $$77875 = 5^3.623;$$

therefore their G. C. M. $= 5^3$,

and their least common multiple $= \dfrac{2^4.5^4 \times 5^3.623}{5^3}$,

$$= 6230000.$$

Hence the least common multiple of 10 and 77·875 is 6230, and the number required $= \dfrac{6230}{77{\cdot}875} = 80$.

1848. (*A*). Prove the rules for finding the greatest common measure and least common multiple of two integers.

(*B*). Find the least number of pounds which can be paid in either half-crowns or guineas.

Here (B) is an example of finding the least common multiple of three numbers.

Reducing pounds, half-crowns, and guineas to sixpences, we have to find the least common multiple of 40, 5, and 42.

Now L. C. M. of 5 and 42 $= 5 \times 42 = 210$, and L. C. M. of 40, 5, and 42 = L. C. M. of 40 and 210

$$= \frac{40 \times 210}{\text{G. C. M. of } 40 \text{ and } 210},$$

$$= \frac{40 \times 210}{10},$$

$$= 840.$$

Therefore least number of pounds required $= \dfrac{840}{40} = 21$.

1850. (A). If a quantity vary directly as a when b is invariable, and inversely as b when a is invariable; prove that it will vary as $\dfrac{a}{b}$ when both a and b are variable.

(B). If 5 men and 7 boys can reap a field of corn of 125 acres in 15 days, in how many days will 10 men and 3 boys reap a field of corn of 75 acres, each boy's work being $\frac{1}{3}$ of a man's?

Since each boy's work is $\frac{1}{3}$ of a man's, therefore 5 men and 7 boys are equivalent to $(5 + \frac{7}{3})$ men, or $\frac{22}{3}$ men; and 10 men and 3 boys are equivalent to $(10 + 1)$ men, or 11 men.

Again, since a given number of men will do more work in proportion as the time is increased; and a given piece of work will require more men to do it in proportion as the time allowed them is *diminished;* therefore

$$\text{days} \propto \text{acres, men given,}$$

$$\text{days} \propto \frac{1}{\text{men}}, \text{ acres given;}$$

therefore, by (A), days $\propto \dfrac{\text{acres}}{\text{men}}$, where men and acres both vary.

But the question gives that when the days = 15 and acres = 125, the men = $\frac{22}{3}$; and we have to find the days when acres = 75 and men = 11.

$$\text{Hence } \frac{\text{days required}}{15} = \frac{\dfrac{75}{11}}{\dfrac{125}{\dfrac{22}{3}}} = \frac{22 \times 75}{3 \times 11 \times 125} = \frac{2}{5}.$$

Therefore days required = 6.

1848. (A). If $A \propto B$ when C is constant, and $A \propto C$ when B is constant; prove that $A \propto BC$, when B and C both vary.

(B). Given that the area of an ellipse varies as either axis when the other is constant, and that the area of a circle of radius unity = 3·14..., find the area of the ellipse whose axes are 3 and 5.

Let a, b be the semi-axes of the ellipse. Then, if A be the area of the ellipse,

$$A \propto a, \ b \text{ constant},$$

and $$A \propto b, \ a \text{ constant},$$

therefore, by (A), $$A \propto ab, \ a, b, \text{ both variable},$$
$$= p.ab, \text{ suppose.}$$

Let $a = b = 1$; then A becomes the area of a circle whose radius is unity;

$$\therefore \ 3·14... = p;$$
$$\therefore \ A = (3·14...)\, ab.$$

Now $$a = \tfrac{3}{2}, \quad b = \tfrac{5}{2}.$$

Therefore $$A = (3·14...)\, \tfrac{15}{4},$$
$$= 11·77...$$

1851. (A). Find the sum of a series of quantities in arithmetical progression.

(B). The square of the arithmetic mean of two quantities is equal to the arithmetic mean of the arithmetic and geometric means of the squares of the same two quantities.

We find from (A), if a be first term of the series, c the last, and n number of terms,

$$\text{sum} = \tfrac{1}{2}n(a+c).$$

Let there be three terms a, b, c of the progression. Then

$$a+b+c = \tfrac{3}{2}(a+c),$$

therefore $$b = \tfrac{3}{2}(a+c) - (a+c) = \frac{a+c}{2};$$

$$\therefore\ b^2 = \tfrac{1}{4}(a^2+c^2+2ac),$$

$$= \tfrac{1}{2}\left(\frac{a^2+c^2}{2} + \sqrt{a^2c^2}\right),$$

$= \text{arithmetic mean between } \dfrac{a^2+c^2}{2},\ \sqrt{a^2c^2}$, *i.e.* between the arithmetic and geometric means of a^2, c^2.

1850. (A). Find the sum of a series of quantities in geometrical progression.

(B). Apply the result to find a common fraction equivalent to a recurring decimal fraction.

(C). If a be the first and l the last of a series of n quantities in geometrical progression, prove that the continued product of the terms of the series is $(al)^{\frac{1}{2}n}$.

(B). Let $\cdot PPP\ldots$ be the recurring decimal, where P, the recurring part, contains p digits. The decimal may be written

$$\frac{P}{10^p} + \frac{P}{10^{2p}} + \frac{P}{10^{3p}} + \ldots\text{ in infinitum.}$$

Now we have from (A), if a be the first term, and r the common ratio of the series,

$$\text{sum of } n \text{ terms} = a\,\frac{r^n-1}{r-1},$$

and if n is indefinitely great and $r<1$,

$$\text{the sum becomes } \frac{a}{1-r}.$$

Hence we have

$$\cdot PPP\ldots = \frac{\frac{P}{10^p}}{1 - \frac{1}{10^p}} = \frac{P}{10^p - 1}.$$

(*C*). The series may be written in the two following ways:

$$a, \quad ar, \quad ar^2, \ldots\ldots ar^{n-1},$$

and
$$l, \quad \frac{l}{r}, \quad \frac{l}{r^2}, \ldots\ldots \frac{l}{r^{n-1}}.$$

Multiplying *all* these $2n$ terms into one another, the result is

$$(al).(al).(al) \ldots\ldots \text{ to } n \text{ terms}$$
$$= (al)^n.$$

Hence the product of the n terms of the series,

= square root of the above result,

$= (al)^{\frac{1}{2}n}$.

1848. (*A*). Find the sum to n terms of a geometric series. What is meant by the sum of an infinite series?

(*B*). If P be the sum of the series formed by taking the 1st and every p^{th} term of an infinite geometric series whose first term is 1, and whose common ratio is < 1, Q the sum of the series formed by taking the 1st and every q^{th} term; prove that

$$P^q.(Q-1)^p = Q^p.(P-1)^q.$$

If r be the common ratio of an infinite geometric series, then, provided $r < 1$, the series has a sum $= \dfrac{1}{1-r}$.

Hence, by the conditions of (*B*), r being the common ratio of the series there mentioned,

$$P = 1 + r^p + r^{2p} + \ldots\ldots \text{ in inf.}$$
$$= \frac{1}{1 - r^p}.$$

$$Q = 1 + r^q + r^{2q} + \ldots\ldots \text{ in inf.}$$

$$= \frac{1}{1 - r^q};$$

therefore $$r^p = \frac{P-1}{P},$$

$$r^q = \frac{Q-1}{Q};$$

whence $$\frac{(Q-1)^p}{Q^p} = r^{pq} = \frac{(P-1)^q}{P^q},$$

or $$P^q.(Q-1)^p = Q^p.(P-1)^q.$$

1851. (*A*). In every geometrical series continued to infinity, each term bears a constant ratio to the sum of all that follow.

(*B*). Find a series in which each term is n times the sum of all that follow it.

From (*A*) we obtain that, if r be the common ratio, any term : sum of all that follow $= \frac{1}{r} - 1$.

In (*B*) we have to find r when the ratio of any term to the sum of all the succeeding terms $= n$, or

$$\frac{1}{r} - 1 = n,$$

therefore $$\frac{1}{r} = n + 1,$$

and $$r = \frac{1}{n+1}.$$

Therefore the series required is

$$a, \frac{a}{n+1}, \frac{a}{(n+1)^2}, \frac{a}{(n+1)^3}, \ldots\ldots \text{ in infinitum},$$

where a may have any value we please.

1849. (*A*). Sum the series $1^3 + 2^3 + 3^3 + \ldots\ldots + n^3$.

(*B*). Prove that when n is indefinitely increased, the fraction $\dfrac{1^p + 2^p + \ldots n^p}{n^{p+1}}$ approaches to $\dfrac{1}{p+1}$ as its limit.

Let $1^p + 2^p + 3^p + \ldots + n^p = A_1 n + A_2 n^2 + \ldots + A_p n^p + A_{p+1} n^{p+1} + \ldots,$

$$\therefore\ 1^p + 2^p + 3^p + \ldots + n^p + (n+1) = A_1 (n+1) + A_2 (n+1)^2 + \ldots$$
$$\ldots + A_p (n+1)^p + A_{p+1} (n+1)^{p+1} + \ldots\ldots$$

Subtracting:

$$(n+1)^p = A_1 \{(n+1) - n\} + A_2 \{(n+1)^2 - n^2\} + \ldots\ldots$$
$$+ A_{p+1} \{(n+1)^{p+1} - n^{p+1}\} + \ldots\ldots$$
$$= A_1 + A_2 \{2n+1) + \ldots + A_{p+1} \{(p+1) . n^p + \ldots\} + \ldots$$

Equating coefficients of n and its powers:

$$1 = A_1 + A_2 + \ldots\ldots + A_{p+1} + \ldots\ldots$$
$$p = 2A_2 + 3A_3 + \ldots\ldots$$
&c. ....
$$1 = (p+1) . A_{p+1} + (p+2) . \frac{p+1}{2} . A_{p+2} + \ldots\ldots$$
$$0 = (p+2) . A_{p+2} + \ldots\ldots$$
&c. ....

These equations will manifestly be satisfied by supposing

$$A_{p+2},\ A_{p+3},\ \text{\&c.} \ldots \text{ each} = 0.$$

Hence
$$1 = (p+1)\ A_{p+1};$$
$$\therefore\ A_{p+1} = \frac{1}{p+1}.$$

We then have

$$\frac{1^p + 2^p + \ldots + n^p}{n^{p+1}} = \frac{A_1}{n^p} + \frac{A_2}{n^{p-1}} + \ldots + \frac{A_p}{n} + A_{p+1},$$

and therefore
$$\text{limit} \left(\frac{1^p + 2^p + \ldots + n^p}{n^{p+1}}\right)_{n=\infty} = A_{p+1},$$
$$= \frac{1}{p+1}.$$

1849. (*A*). Find the number of combinations of n things taken r together.

(*B*). There are n points in a plane, no three of which are in the same straight line, with the exception of p, which are in the same straight line; find the number of lines which result from joining them.

If no three of the points were in the same straight line, the number of lines formed by joining them would be the number of combinations of n things taken r together, *i.e.*

$$\frac{n.(n-1)}{1.2}, \text{ by } (A).$$

Similarly, considering the p points only, and supposing no three of them in the same straight line, the number of lines formed by joining them would be

$$\frac{p.(p-1)}{1.2}.$$

But, since all the p points are in the same straight line, all these $\frac{p(p-1)}{1.2}$ lines are merged into one only.

Hence, if x is the number required,

$$x - 1 + \frac{p.(p-1)}{1.2} = \frac{n.(n-1)}{1.2}.$$

Therefore $$x = \frac{n(n-1)}{1.2} - \frac{p.(p-1)}{1.2} + 1,$$

$$= \frac{(n-p)(n+p-1)}{2} + 1.$$

1850. (*A*). Find an expression for the amount of a given sum of money which has accumulated during a given number of years at a given rate of compound interest.

(*B*). If a sum of money, at a given rate of compound interest, accumulate to p-fold its original value in n years, and to p'-fold its original value in n' years; prove that

$$n' = n.\log_p p'.$$

The result of (A) is $M = PR^n$, where R = £1, together with the interest on £1 for 1 year.

By the first condition of (B) we have

$$pP = P.R^n,$$

or $$p = R^n \text{.............................}(1).$$

By second condition, $$p'P = PR^{n'},$$

or $$p' = R^{n'} \text{..........................} (2).$$

From (1), $$1 = n \log_p R,$$

from (2), $$\log_p p' = n'.\log_p R;$$

therefore $$\frac{n'}{n} = \log_p p',$$

or $$n' = n \log_p p'.$$

1851. (A). If interest be payable every instant, and the interest for one year be an mth part of the principal, find the amount for any number of years.

(B). If a quantity change continuously in value from a to b in a given time t_1, the increase at any time bearing a constant ratio to its value at that time, prove that its value at any time t will be $a\left(\frac{b}{a}\right)^{\frac{t}{t_1}}$.

If in (A) P be the principal, M the amount, n the number of years,

$$M = P\left(1 + \frac{1}{m}\right)^n.$$

The problem (A) involves a principle which need not be restricted to the idea of interest. We may regard a sum of money put out at compound interest, which is due every instant, as the type of a varying quantity which increases continuously from one value to another. Now in (B) all the conditions are satisfied for the varying quantity, which hold for the sum of money in (A) which is put out to interest. Therefore the above result must hold for the varying quantity in (B).

Here $P = a$; and $M = b$, when $n = t_1$, the unit of time being arbitrary; and the constant ratio $= \dfrac{1}{m+1}$.

Therefore
$$b = a\left(1 + \frac{1}{m}\right)^{t_1} \ldots\ldots\ldots\ldots\ldots\ldots\ldots (1),$$

and if x is the required value at the time t,
$$x = a\left(1 + \frac{1}{m}\right)^{t} \ldots\ldots\ldots\ldots\ldots\ldots\ldots (2).$$

From (1),
$$1 + \frac{1}{m} = \left(\frac{b}{a}\right)^{\frac{1}{t_1}},$$

therefore
$$x = a\left(\frac{b}{a}\right)^{\frac{t}{t_1}}.$$

1850. (A). Express the number of numbers less than a given number which are prime to it, in terms of the given number and its prime factors.

(B). Shew that the sum of these numbers is equal to half the product of the number of them into the given number.

From (A) we find that the number of numbers prime to and less than $N = N\left(\dfrac{a-1}{a}\right) \cdot \left(\dfrac{b-1}{b}\right) \ldots\ldots$ where $a, b, \ldots\ldots$ are the prime factors of N.

(1). Let $N = a^m$. Then the numbers $< N$ and not prime to it are
$$a,\ 2a,\ 3a, \ldots\ldots a^{m-1}.\, a,$$

the sum of which $= \dfrac{a^{m-1}}{2}(a + a^m)$,
$$= \frac{N(N+a)}{2a}.$$

therefore sum of numbers $< N$ and prime to N

$$= \frac{N(N+1)}{2} - \frac{N(N+a)}{2a}$$

$$= \frac{N}{2a}(Na - N)$$

$$= \frac{N}{2} N\left(\frac{a-1}{a}\right)$$

$$= \frac{N}{2} \times \text{number of numbers less than } N \text{ and prime to it.}$$

(2). Let $N = a^m b^n$,

then, the numbers divisible by a and $< N$ are

$$a,\ 2a,\ 3a,\ \ldots\ldots\ a^{m-1}b^n a,$$

those divisible by b are

$$b,\ 2b,\ 3b,\ \ldots\ldots\ a^m b^{n-1} b,$$

those divisible by ab are

$$ab,\ 2ab,\ 3ab,\ \ldots\ldots\ a^{m-1}b^{n-1}ab.$$

Hence, observing that each of the two former sets include the latter, the sum of all numbers less than N and not prime to it, is

$$\frac{a^{m-1}b^n}{2}(a + a^m b^n) + \frac{a^m b^{n-1}}{2}(b + a^m b^n) - \frac{a^{m-1}b^{n-1}}{2}(ab + a^m b^n)$$

$$= \frac{N(N+a)}{2a} + \frac{N(N+b)}{2b} - \frac{N(N+ab)}{2ab}$$

$$= \frac{N}{2ab}\{N(a+b) - N + ab\};$$

therefore sum of the numbers $< N$ and prime to it

$$= \frac{N(N+1)}{2} - \frac{N}{2ab}\{N(a+b) - N + ab\}$$

$$= \frac{N^2}{2} \frac{ab - a - b + 1}{ab}$$

$$= \frac{N}{2} \times N\left(\frac{a-1}{a}\right)\left(\frac{b-1}{b}\right),$$

and so on for more factors.

TRIGONOMETRY.

1851. (*A*). Compare the magnitudes of two angles which contain the same number of French and English degrees respectively.

(*B*). Divide an angle which contains n degrees into two parts, one of which contains as many English minutes as the other does French.

From (*A*) we get, that if A and B be two angles of which the former contains as many English degrees as the latter does French grades,

$$\frac{A}{B} = \frac{10}{9}.$$

If A contained as many English *minutes* as B contains French, the above formula would have to be modified into

$$\frac{A}{B} = \frac{10}{9} \times \frac{100}{60} = \frac{50}{27}.$$

Let now A, B be the two required parts of the given angle, expressed in English degrees. Then we have

$$A + B = n;$$

therefore $$A\left(1 + \tfrac{27}{50}\right) = n;$$

therefore $$A = \tfrac{50}{77}n,$$

and $$B = \tfrac{27}{77}n.$$

1849. (*A*). Define the cosine of an angle; and trace its changes in sign and magnitude as the angle increases from $135°$ to $405°$.

(*B*) Construct the angle whose tangent is $3 - \sqrt{2}$.

In the investigation of (A), we prove that

$$\cos 45^\circ = \frac{1}{\sqrt{2}}.$$

Take any finite straight line AB (fig. 28). Draw BC at right angles to AB and $= 3AB$.

Make $BD = AB$ and join AD. Cut off from CB, $CE = AD$, and join AE. BAE shall be the angle required.

For, since $BD = AB$, the $\angle BAD = 45^\circ$;

therefore $$\frac{AB}{AD} = \cos 45^\circ = \frac{1}{\sqrt{2}};$$

therefore $$AD = \sqrt{2}\, AB.$$

Hence $$\begin{aligned} BE &= BC - CE \\ &= BC - AD \\ &= 3AB - \sqrt{2}.AB; \end{aligned}$$

therefore $$\tan BAE = \frac{BE}{AB} = 3 - \sqrt{2};$$

or BAE is the angle required.

1851. (A). Prove that $\sin(A+B) = \sin A \cos B + \cos A \sin B$, and deduce a similar expression for $\cos(A+B)$.

(B). If $a \tan A + b \tan B = (a+b) \tan \dfrac{A+B}{2}$,

shew that $$\frac{a}{b} = \frac{\cos A}{\cos B}.$$

From the given equation

$$a\left(\tan A - \tan\frac{A+B}{2}\right) = b\left(\tan\frac{A+B}{2} - \tan B\right);$$

$$\therefore \frac{a}{\cos A}\left(\sin A \cos\frac{A+B}{2} - \cos A \sin\frac{A+B}{2}\right)$$
$$= \frac{b}{\cos B}\left(\sin\frac{A+B}{2}\cos B - \cos\frac{A+B}{2}\sin B\right).$$

But by (A),

$$\sin A \cos\frac{A+B}{2} - \cos A \sin\frac{A+B}{2} = \sin\left(A - \frac{A+B}{2}\right) = \sin\frac{A-B}{2},$$

and $\sin\frac{A+B}{2}\cos B - \cos\frac{A+B}{2}\sin B = \sin\left(\frac{A+B}{2} - B\right) = \sin\frac{A-B}{2}$;

therefore
$$\frac{a}{\cos A} = \frac{b}{\cos B},$$

or
$$\frac{a}{b} = \frac{\cos A}{\cos B}.$$

1848. (A). Express $\sin 2A$ in terms of $\tan A$.

(B). Given $\tan\frac{1}{2}A = 2 - \sqrt{3}$, find $\sin A$, and thence A.

From (A), we have
$$\sin 2A = \frac{2\tan A}{1+\tan^2 A};$$

therefore
$$\sin A = \frac{2\tan\frac{1}{2}A}{1+\tan^2\frac{1}{2}A}$$
$$= \frac{2(2-\sqrt{3})}{1+7-4\sqrt{3}}$$
$$= \frac{2(2-\sqrt{3})}{4(2-\sqrt{3})}$$
$$= \tfrac{1}{2};$$

therefore
$$A = 30^\circ.$$

1850. (A). If $A + B + C = 180^\circ$, prove that
$$\tan A + \tan B + \tan C = \tan A \tan B \tan C.$$

(B). If α, β, γ, denote the distances from the angular points of a triangle, to the points of contact of the inscribed circle, shew that the radius of the inscribed circle
$$= \left(\frac{\alpha\beta\gamma}{\alpha+\beta+\gamma}\right)^{\frac{1}{2}}.$$

Here (B) is a direct application of the formula proved in (A).

If O (fig. 29) is the centre of an inscribed circle, the lines OA, OB, OC, bisect angles A, B, C.

Hence the $\angle B'OC' = 2\angle B'OA'$

$$= 2A' \text{ suppose},$$

$$\angle C'OA' = 2B',$$

$$\angle A'OB' = 2C'.$$

Now $\angle B'OC' + \angle C'OA' + \angle A'OB' = 360°$;

therefore $A' + B' + C' = 180°$.

Let $OA' = r = OB' = OC'$.

We have also

$$AB' = AC' = \alpha,$$

$$BC' = BA' = \beta,$$

$$CA' = CB' = \gamma,$$

and the geometry of the figure gives

$$\alpha = r\tan A', \quad \beta = r\tan B', \quad \gamma = r\tan C';$$

therefore $\alpha\beta\gamma = r^3 \tan A' \tan B' \tan C'$,

$$\alpha + \beta + \gamma = r\{\tan A' + \tan B' + \tan C'\}$$

$$= r\tan A' \tan B' \tan C',$$

since A', B', C', fulfil the condition of (A);

therefore $r^2 = \dfrac{\alpha\beta\gamma}{\alpha+\beta+\gamma}$,

and $r = \left(\dfrac{\alpha\beta\gamma}{\alpha+\beta+\gamma}\right)^{\frac{1}{2}}$.

1848. (A). Prove that the sines of the angles of a triangle are proportional to the opposite sides.

(B). Hence deduce the expression for the cosine of an angle in terms of the sides.

From (A) $\dfrac{\sin A}{a} = \dfrac{\sin B}{b} = \dfrac{\sin C}{c} = r$, suppose;

therefore $\sin A = ar, \quad \sin B = br, \quad \sin C = cr$,

and $\cos A = \sqrt{(1-a^2r^2)}, \quad \cos B = \sqrt{(1-b^2r^2)}, \quad \cos C = \sqrt{(1-c^2r^2)}$.

Now in every triangle,

$$A + B + C = 180^\circ;$$

therefore $\sin(A+B) = \sin(180^\circ - C) = \sin C$,

or $\sin A \cos B + \cos A \sin B = \sin C$.

Substituting for $\sin A$, $\cos B$, &c.,

$$ar\sqrt{(1-b^2r^2)} + br\sqrt{(1-a^2r^2)} = cr,$$

or $a\sqrt{(1-b^2r^2)} = c - b\sqrt{(1-a^2r^2)}$.

Squaring, $a^2 - a^2b^2r^2 = c^2 + b^2 - a^2b^2r^2 - 2bc\sqrt{(1-a^2r^2)}$;

therefore $a^2 = c^2 + b^2 - 2bc\sqrt{(1-a^2r^2)}$,

therefore

$$\cos A = \sqrt{(1-a^2r^2)} = \frac{b^2+c^2-a^2}{2bc}.$$

1850. (*A*). If a, b, c, be the sides of a triangle, prove that its area is equal to

$$\tfrac{1}{4}\sqrt{(2b^2c^2 + 2c^2a^2 + 2a^2b^2 - a^4 - b^4 - c^4)}.$$

(*B*). Apply this expression to find the area when the angle opposite to c is a right angle.

When the angle opposite to c is a right angle,

$$c^2 = a^2 + b^2;$$

$$\begin{aligned} \therefore\ 2b^2c^2 + 2c^2a^2 + 2a^2b^2 - a^4 - b^4 - c^4 &= 2c^4 + 2a^2b^2 - a^4 - b^4 - c^4 \\ &= c^4 - (a^2-b^2)^2 \\ &= (a^2+b^2)^2 - (a^2-b^2)^2 \\ &= 4a^2b^2; \end{aligned}$$

hence area required $= \tfrac{1}{2}ab$.

1850. (*A*). Shew that in general it will be possible to determine two triangles in which two sides and the angle opposite to the less are of given magnitudes.

(*B*). If a, b, B, be given, and a be $> b$, and if c, c' be the two values found for the third side of the triangle, then

$$c^2 - 2cc'\cos 2B + c'^2 = 4b^2\cos^2 B.$$

c, c' are the two roots of the equation

$$b^2 = a^2 + c^2 - 2ac\cos B,$$

or
$$c^2 - 2ac\cos B + a^2 - b^2 = 0.$$

Hence
$$cc' = a^2 - b^2,$$
$$c + c' = 2a\cos B;$$

therefore
$$c^2 + 2cc' + c'^2 = 4a^2\cos^2 B$$
$$= 4(cc' + b^2)\cos^2 B,$$

or observing that
$$2\cos^2 B - 1 = \cos 2B,$$
$$c^2 - 2cc'\cos 2B + c'^2 = 4b^2\cos^2 B.$$

1849. (A). Two sides and the included angle of a triangle being given, shew how to find the remaining angles.

(B). The ratio of two sides of a triangle is 9 : 7, and the included angle is 47°.25′; find the other angles. Given
$$\log 2 = \cdot 3010300,$$
$$L\tan 66°.17'.30'' = 10\cdot 3573942,$$
$$L\tan 15°.53' = 9\cdot 4541479;\ \text{diff. } 1' = 4797.$$

Let C, a, b, be the given parts. Then the equations

$$\frac{A+B}{2} = 90° - \frac{C}{2}$$

and
$$\tan\frac{A-B}{2} = \frac{a-b}{a+b}\cot\frac{C}{2}$$

determine $\frac{A+B}{2}$ and $\frac{A-B}{2}$; and therefore

$$A = \frac{A+B}{2} + \frac{A-B}{2},$$
$$B = \frac{A+B}{2} - \frac{A-B}{2}$$

are known.

Here we have
$$C = 47°.25',\quad \frac{a}{b} = \frac{9}{7};$$

therefore
$$\frac{A+B}{2} = 90° - 23°.42'.30''$$
$$= 66°.17'.30'',$$

and $$\frac{a-b}{a+b} = \frac{9-7}{9+7} = \frac{2}{16} = \frac{1}{8};$$

therefore $$\tan\frac{A-B}{2} = \frac{1}{8}\cot 23^\circ.42'.30''$$

$$= \frac{1}{2^3}\tan 66^\circ.17'.30'';$$

therefore $$L\tan\frac{A-B}{2} = L\tan 66^\circ.17'.30'' - 3\log 2$$

$$= 10{\cdot}3573942 - {\cdot}9030900$$

$$= 9{\cdot}4543042$$

$$= L\tan(15^\circ.53' + \delta'') \text{ suppose.}$$

Now the rule of proportional parts gives (if consecutive angles in the tables differ by 1')

$$\frac{\delta}{60} = \frac{L\tan(15^\circ.53'+\delta'') - L\tan 15^\circ.53'}{L\tan 15^\circ.54' - L\tan 15^\circ.53'}$$

$$= \tfrac{1563}{4797};$$

therefore $$\delta = 20.\tfrac{1563}{1599} = 19''.5.$$

Hence $$\frac{A-B}{2} = 15^\circ.53'.19''.5;$$

therefore $A = 66^\circ.17'.30'' + 15^\circ.53'.19''.5 = 82^\circ.10'.49''.5$,

$B = 66^\circ.17'.30'' - 15^\circ.53'.19''.5 = 50^\circ.24'.10''.5$.

1848. (*A*). Express the area of a triangle in terms (1) of two sides and the contained angle (2) of one side and the adjacent angles.

(*B*). Two sides of a triangle are equal to 3 and 12 respectively, and the contained angle is equal to 30°: find the hypothenuse of an equal right-angled isosceles triangle.

The area of a triangle ABC

$$= \tfrac{1}{2}ab\sin C \text{..........................(1)},$$

and $$= \frac{c^2}{2}\cdot\frac{\sin A\sin B}{\sin(A+B)} \text{..................(2).}$$

In the first-mentioned triangle of (B), we have

$$a = 3, \quad b = 12, \quad C = 30^\circ;$$

therefore

$$\text{its area} = \tfrac{1}{2}.3.12 \sin 30^\circ$$
$$= 3.6.\tfrac{1}{2}$$
$$= 9.$$

In the right-angled isosceles triangle, we have

$$A = B = 45^\circ,$$

therefore

$$\text{its area} = \frac{c^2}{2} \sin^2 45$$
$$= \frac{c^2}{2} \tfrac{1}{2}$$
$$= \frac{c^2}{4}.$$

But the areas of the two triangles are to be equal, therefore

$$\frac{c^2}{4} = 9,$$

or

$$c = 6.$$

1849. (A). Shew how to find the height of an object above a horizontal plane from observations made at two given stations in the plane.

(B). The angular elevation of a tower at a place A due south of it is 30°, and at a place B, due west of A, and at a distance a from it the elevation is 18°: shew that the height of the tower is

$$\frac{a}{\sqrt{(2\sqrt{5} + 2)}}.$$

If in (A), OC (fig. 30) be the tower, A, B the two stations, the angles OAC, OBC will be known from observation, and the distance AB and the angle CAB will be known because the stations are known.

CA, CB can each be expressed in terms of OC from the triangles AOC, BOC; and therefore a relation can be found between CA and CB. Another relation between them is given by the triangle ABC. We thus are able to find CA or CB, and thence OC.

In (B) we have given that

$$\angle OAC = 30^\circ, \quad \angle OBC = 18^\circ, \quad \angle CAB = 90^\circ, \quad \text{and } AB = a.$$

Let $$OC = x, \quad CA = y, \quad CB = y',$$

then $$x = y \tan 30^\circ,$$

and $$x = y' \tan 18^\circ;$$

therefore $$y' \tan 18^\circ = y \tan 30^\circ \text{..................... (1)}.$$

Also from the right-angled triangle ABC,

$$y'^2 = y^2 + a^2 \text{........................ (2)};$$

therefore $$y^2 \left(\frac{\tan^2 30^\circ}{\tan^2 18^\circ} - 1\right) = a^2,$$

or $$y = \frac{a \tan 18^\circ}{\sqrt{(\tan^2 30^\circ - \tan^2 18)}};$$

therefore $$x = \frac{a \tan 18^\circ \tan 30^\circ}{\sqrt{(\tan^2 30^\circ - \tan^2 18^\circ)}}$$

$$= \frac{a}{\sqrt{(\cot^2 18 - \cot^2 30^\circ)}}.$$

Now $$\cot 30^\circ = \sqrt{3}, \quad \cot 18^\circ = \frac{\sqrt{\{2(5+\sqrt{5})\}}}{\sqrt{5}-1};$$

therefore $$\cot^2 18^\circ - \cot^2 30^\circ = \frac{5+\sqrt{5}}{3-\sqrt{5}} - 3$$

$$= \frac{4(\sqrt{5}-1)}{3-\sqrt{5}}$$

$$= \frac{8(\sqrt{5}-1)}{(\sqrt{5}-1)^2}$$

$$= \frac{2(\sqrt{5}-1)(\sqrt{5}+1)}{\sqrt{5}-1}$$

$$= 2\sqrt{5} + 2;$$

therefore $$x = \frac{a}{\sqrt{(2\sqrt{5}+2)}}.$$

1848. (*A*). Shew how to determine the height of a mountain by observations at two stations in the same horizontal plane, the distance between the stations being known.

(*B*). If the stations are in the same vertical plane passing through the summit, and the summit (S) is observed from the further station, but a lower point (S') is observed by mistake from the nearer, shew that the height determined by the process lies between the heights of S and S'.

The process of finding the height of the mountain would in this case be to observe the angle NAS (fig. 31) from the further station A, and the $\angle N'BS'$ from the nearer station, and, knowing the distance AB, to determine the height (x) from the triangles ASN, $BS'N'$ on the supposition that SN, $S'N'$ were each $= x$; the result obtained would correspond to the height $S''N''$ of the point where BS' produced meets AS; and since S is supposed to be invisible at B, S'' must be lower than S but higher than S'.

STATICS.

1848. (*A*). If two forces, acting on a particle, be represented by two adjacent sides of a parallelogram, prove that their resultant will act in the direction of the corresponding diagonal.

(*B*). Explain how the force of the current may be taken advantage of to urge a ferry-boat across a river, the centre of the boat being attached, by means of a long rope, to a mooring in the middle of a stream.

Let the boat be kept in a position inclined to the direction of the stream at an angle of about 45°, its foremost end pointing up the stream. The current will produce upon the boat a pressure consisting of two parts, one perpendicular to the side of the boat, the other in the direction of its length. The latter is inconsiderable compared with the former, because the surface offered to the perpendicular resistance is much greater than that which the longitudinal pressure acts upon. Considering the rope (since it is long) as nearly parallel to the direction of the stream, we shall have two forces, viz. the tension of the rope and the pressure of the water perpendicular to the side of the boat, the resultant of which, by the proposition, acts between them, and therefore tends to propel the boat towards the bank, to which the foremost end of the boat is directed.

1849. (*A*). Assuming the parallelogram of forces, so far as the direction of the resultant is concerned, shew that the diagonal of the parallelogram represents the magnitude of the resultant.

(*B*). The resultant of two forces is 10 lbs., one of them is equal to 8 lbs., and the direction of the other is inclined to the resultant at an angle of 36°: find the other force, and the angle between the two.

Let OA, OB, (fig. 32) represent the two forces; then, by (A), OC, the diagonal of the parallelogram $OACB$, represents their resultant.

We have given OA proportional to 8, OC to 10, and OB to x (the number of lbs. in the required force); and $\angle BOC = 36°$.

From the triangle OAC,

$$OA^2 = OC^2 + AC^2 - 2\,OC.AC\cos OCA;$$

therefore $$8^2 = 10^2 + x^2 - 2.10\,x\cos 36°,$$

or $$64 = 100 + x^2 - 2.10.x\,\frac{\sqrt{5}+1}{4};$$

therefore $$x^2 - 5(\sqrt{5}+1)\,x + 36 = 0,$$

which gives x.

Also, $$\begin{aligned}\sin AOB &= \sin OAC \\ &= \frac{OC}{OA}\sin OCA \\ &= \tfrac{10}{8}\sin 36° \\ &= \tfrac{5}{4}\sin 36°,\end{aligned}$$

which gives the angle AOB.

1850. (A). If three forces which act in a plane keep a rigid body at rest, prove that their lines of action are either parallel or pass through a point; and in both cases, shew that any two of the forces are inversely proportional to the perpendiculars drawn on their respective lines of action from any point in the line of action of the third.

(B). An uniform heavy rod of given length is to be supported in a given position with its upper end resting at a given point against a smooth vertical wall, by means of a fine string attached to the lower end of the rod and to a point in the wall. Find by geometrical construction the point in the wall to which the string must be attached.

Let AB (fig. 33) be the rod, G (its middle point) its centre of gravity; the forces which keep it at rest are

its weight acting along GW,

tension of string along BP,

and reaction of wall along $AR \perp NP$.

Now the principle of which (A) is the enunciation tells us that these three forces must meet in a point (because they are not parallel) in order that there may be equilibrium. We must therefore suppose the string BP placed in such a position that it shall pass through O the intersection of AR and WG produced. When this is done, all the statical conditions have been brought in, and the problem of finding the *position* of equilibrium is solely a *geometrical* one.

We have then from the geometry of the figure,

$$AP : AN :: PO : OB :: AG : GB.$$

But $$AG = GB;$$

therefore $$AP = AN.$$

Since the position and length of AB is given, AN is known, and therefore the point P where the string is to be tied, is determined by taking $AP = AN$.

1848. (A). When a body is kept in equilibrium by three forces acting in one plane, either their directions are parallel, and one force is equal to the sum or difference of the other two; or their directions meet in a point, and each force is as the sine of the angle between the other two.

(B). AB is a rod capable of turning freely about its extremity A, which is fixed; CD is another rod equal to $2AB$, and attached at its middle point to the extremity B of the former, so as to turn freely about this point; a given force acts at C in the direction CA: find the force which must be applied at D in order to produce equilibrium.

Let F be the given force acting along CA (fig. 34), the pressure (R) at the hinge B or the rod CD must act along AB; for if it does not, the equal reaction upon the rod AB would make it revolve about A, and equilibrium would not exist. We have now the rigid body CD acted on by two forces F and R, whose directions pass through A; the force (P) therefore which, acting at D, is to preserve the equilibrium, must, by (A), also pass through A.

The proposition further tells us that the magnitude of each of the forces P, F, R, is proportional to the sine of the angle between the other two. Hence

$$P : F : R :: \sin BAC : \sin BAD : \sin CAD;$$

therefore
$$\frac{P}{F} = \frac{\sin BAC}{\sin BAD}.$$

But since
$$AB = BC = BD,$$
$$\sin BAC = \cos \tfrac{1}{2} ABC,$$
and
$$\sin BAD = \sin \tfrac{1}{2} ABC;$$
therefore
$$P = F \frac{\cos \frac{1}{2} ABC}{\sin \frac{1}{2} ABC}$$
$$= F \cot \tfrac{1}{2} ABC.$$

1848. (A). Assuming the principle of the straight lever for two forces, find the condition of equilibrium of a rigid body moveable about a fixed axis, and acted on by any number of forces in a plane perpendicular to the axis.

(B). If a set of forces, acting at the angular points of a plane polygon, be represented by the sides, taken in order, shew that their tendency to turn a body about an axis perpendicular to the plane of the polygon is the same through whatever point of the plane the axis passes.

The result obtained in (A) is that the sum of the moments about the fixed axis of all the forces which tend to turn the body one way round must be equal to the sum of the moments of all the forces which tend to turn it the opposite way round. This condition expresses nothing more than the fact, that the moment of any force about the fixed axis is a proper measure of its tendency to turn the body round the axis.

Let now *ABDF* (fig. 35) be a polygon whose sides represent in magnitude and direction a series of forces tending to turn a body round an axis through *O* perpendicular to the plane of the polygon. The tendency of the force represented by *AB* to turn the body round *O* will be, from above, proportional to its moment about *O*, *i.e.* to $AB.ON$ (ON being $\perp AB$), and therefore proportional to the area of the triangle *AOB*. Hence if, as in fig. 35, *O* be within the polygon, the whole tendency of the forces to turn the body round *O* will be proportional to the area of the polygon, and therefore the same wherever within the polygon *O* may be.

If *O* be without the polygon (fig. 36), we observe that those forces *DE*, *EF*, *FA*, the triangles corresponding to which lie entirely outside the polygon, tend to turn the body in the opposite direction to that in which the forces such as *AB*, *BC*,... tend to turn it. In forming therefore the algebraical sum of the moments, the triangles corresponding to the former forces will have to be *subtracted*, so that the whole tendency of the forces to turn the body round *O* will still be proportional to the area of the polygon, and will therefore be the same whatever be the position of *O*.

1849. (*A*). State and explain the conditions necessary and sufficient for the equilibrium of a body which has one or more points in contact with a smooth plane, and is acted on by any forces.

(*B*). A triangular board of given weight rests in equilibrium with its base on a horizontal plane sufficiently rough to prevent all sliding. A force acts upon it in its own plane and in a given line drawn through the vertex and without the triangle: find by a geometrical construction, or otherwise, the limits between which the magnitude of the force must lie if the equilibrium is preserved.

If one point only of a body be in contact with a smooth plane, the forces acting on the body (excluding the reaction of the plane) must admit of a resultant passing through the point of contact and perpendicular to the plane. If two points are in contact with the plane, the resultant must pass through the line joining them; and, generally, if there be more than two points of contact, it must meet the plane in a point within the polygon formed by joining the points of contact; the direction of the resultant being in all cases perpendicular to the plane, in order that the body may not slide.

In (B), since the plane is sufficiently rough to prevent sliding, the last condition is not necessary; the only condition therefore that in this case is necessary is, that the direction of the resultant of the weight of the triangle and the force which acts at the vertex shall cut the base of the triangle.

Let the vertical through the centre of gravity G (fig. 37) of the triangle meet the given line through A in O, and the base of the triangle in M. Then, in the limiting case of equilibrium, OB must be the direction of the resultant of the weight (W) of the triangle and the force (F) which is to act at A.

Draw $MN \parallel OF$. Since the two forces F, W, and their resultant reversed of course balance, the sides of the triangle OMN, which are in the direction of these forces, must be proportional to their magnitudes. Hence, OM representing the weight of the triangle, MN will represent the greatest value of the force F.

Similarly, if F acts in the direction AO, MN' would represent the greatest possible value of F, where N' is the point of intersection of OC produced and NM produced.

If we wish to put this result into an analytical form, we may assume the angle which OF makes with $CB = \alpha$, $\angle OBM = \theta$.

Then,
$$\frac{F}{W} = \frac{MN}{OM} = \frac{\sin MON}{\sin ONM} = \frac{\cos\theta}{\sin(\theta + \alpha)}.$$

Now θ is known from the geometry. For
$$\sin\theta = \frac{OM}{OB} = \frac{OM}{c} \cdot \frac{\sin(\theta + \alpha)}{\sin(B + \alpha)},$$

using the usual notation for the sides and angles of the triangle ABC. Also

$$\begin{aligned} OM &= AD - MD \,.\, \tan\alpha, \\ &= AD - 2EM \,.\, \tan\alpha, \\ &= c \,.\, \cos B - \tfrac{1}{3}(a - 2c \,.\, \cos B) \,.\, \tan\alpha, \\ &= p, \text{ suppose.} \end{aligned}$$

Making the necessary substitutions, we obtain

$$F = \frac{W}{c} \,.\, \{c \,.\, \operatorname{cosec}\alpha - p \,.\, \cot\alpha \,.\, \operatorname{cosec}(B + \alpha)\}.$$

(B) might also be solved by observing that the moment of F about B must always be not greater than the moment of W about the same point; and in the limiting case these moments must be equal, which consideration immediately gives a value for F.

1849. (A). Explain the nature of the action and reaction of smooth surfaces in contact.

(B). Two equal circular disks with smooth edges, placed on their flat sides in the corner between two smooth vertical planes inclined at a given angle, touch each other in the line bisecting the angle. Find the radius of the least disk which may be pressed between them without causing them to separate.

The mutual pressure of two smooth surfaces in contact acts along the common normal to the surfaces at the point of contact.

Let O_1, O_2 (fig. 38) be the centres of the two disks, N_1, N_2 the points where they touch the walls. Let the radius of either disk $= r$, and the angle between the walls $= 4\alpha$.

Produce N_1O_1, N_2O_2 to meet in O. O will be the centre of the required disk. For if the centre of this third disk be at all nearer to A, *i.e.* if the disk be at all smaller, the lines joining its centre with O_1 and O_2 will meet AN_1 and AN_2 *produced;* and therefore the pressures (which act in these lines) exerted on the two given disks, will tend to push them away from A, and therefore to separate from one another. To find the radius (R) of the third disk, we have

$$\begin{aligned} R &= ON_1 - m_1N_1, \\ &= AN_1 . \tan 2\alpha - 2r, \\ &= r . \cot\alpha . \tan 2\alpha - 2r, \\ &= \frac{2r . \tan^2\alpha}{1 - \tan^2\alpha}, \\ &= r . \tan\alpha . \tan 2\alpha. \end{aligned}$$

1849. (A). Find the centre of gravity of a triangle.

(B). One corner of a triangle, equal to $\frac{1}{n}$th part of its area, is cut off by a line parallel to its base; find the centre of gravity of the remainder.

Let ABC (fig. 39) be the given triangle; $Abc = \frac{1}{n}$ of its area, bc being $\parallel BC$.

From (A) we know that if AD be drawn to the middle point of BC, and take $DG = \frac{1}{3}DA$, G is the centre of gravity of the triangle. Moreover it is proved in the investigation of (A), that AD bisects every line parallel to BC; thus d is the middle point of bc, and therefore if $dg = \frac{1}{3}dA$, g is the centre of gravity of triangle Abc. Let G' be that of $bcCB$.

Since the centre of gravity of a body is that point at which its weight may be supposed to act, G may be considered as the point of application of the resultant of the weights of the portions Abc, $bcCB$. Hence

$$\begin{aligned} GG' : Gg &:: \text{weight of } Abc : \text{weight of } bcCB, \\ &:: \text{area } Abc : \text{area } bcCB, \\ &:: 1 : n - 1; \end{aligned}$$

therefore $$GG' = \frac{Gg}{n-1}.$$

Now $$\begin{aligned} GG' &= GD - G'D, \\ &= \tfrac{1}{3}AD - G'D. \end{aligned}$$

Also, since $n : 1 :: \text{area } ABC : \text{area } Abc :: AD^2 : Ad^2$,

therefore $$Ad = \frac{AD}{\sqrt{n}},$$

and we get $$\begin{aligned} Gg &= AG - Ag, \\ &= 2(AD - Ad), \\ &= 2AD \cdot \left(1 - \frac{1}{\sqrt{n}}\right). \end{aligned}$$

Therefore, substituting in the above relation,

$$\begin{aligned} \tfrac{1}{3}AD - G'D &= 2AD \cdot \frac{\sqrt{n} - 1}{3\sqrt{n}(n-1)}, \\ &= \frac{2AD}{3\sqrt{n}(\sqrt{n}+1)}. \end{aligned}$$

Therefore $$\begin{aligned} G'D &= \tfrac{1}{3}AD - \frac{2AD}{3\sqrt{n} \cdot (\sqrt{n}+1)}, \\ &= \frac{n + \sqrt{n} - 2}{3\sqrt{n} \cdot (\sqrt{n}+1)} AD. \end{aligned}$$

1848. (A). When a weight is supported on a smooth inclined plane by a force along the plane, the force is to the weight as the height of the plane is to its length.

(B). If the roughness of a plane, which is inclined to the horizon at a known angle, be such that a body will just rest supported on it, find the least force along the plane requisite to drag the body up.

In this case we have an extension of the problem (A) to the case where the plane is rough, the roughness being given by the fact that a body would just rest on the plane. This fact shews at once that, if ε be the inclination of the plane to the horizon, the reaction (which must balance the weight of the body) acts at angle ε to the normal to the plane in the opposite direction to that in which the body is on the point of sliding.

Hence, if the body be on the point of sliding *up* the plane under the action of a force (P) along the plane, the reaction (R) will act as in fig. 40, where $\angle NOR$ between its direction and the normal $= \varepsilon$.

Let ML (fig. 40) drawn parallel to OP meet RO produced in L. Then the sides of the triangle OLM, being parallel to the directions of the three forces P, W, R, which keep O at rest, will be proportional to their magnitudes; *i.e.*

$$P : W : R :: ML : OM : OL.$$

Therefore
$$\frac{P}{W} = \frac{ML}{OM},$$
$$= \frac{\sin MOL}{\sin OLM},$$
$$= \frac{\sin 2\varepsilon}{\cos \varepsilon},$$
$$= 2 \sin \varepsilon.$$

Therefore
$$P = 2W . \sin \varepsilon.$$

1850. (A). Find the ratio of the power to the weight necessary for equilibrium on an inclined plane, when the power acts along the plane.

(B). If the inclined plane be the upper surface of a wedge whose under surface rests on a smooth horizontal table, find the horizontal force which must act on the wedge to keep it at rest.

From the equilibrium of the particle O (fig. 41) we have, by the same method as is pursued in (A),

$$R = W . \cos \alpha \text{ .... } (1).$$

From the equilibrium of the wedge, observing that the effect of the particle resting on the wedge is to impress upon it a force R perpendicular to the slant side, we have, by equating horizontal forces,

$$R . \sin \alpha = F \text{ .... } (2);$$

therefore
$$F = W . \sin \alpha . \cos \alpha,$$
$$= \frac{W}{2} . \sin 2\alpha.$$

1850. (*A*). Find the ratio of the power to the weight necessary for equilibrium on the wheel and axle.

(*B*). If the axis about which the machine turns coincide with that of the axle, but not with the axis of the wheel, find the greatest and least ratios of the power and weight necessary for equilibrium, neglecting the weight of the machine.

Let O (fig. 42) be the axis of the axle, O' of the wheel.

$$OA = a, \quad O'B = b, \quad OO' = c.$$

If P be hung at B, W at A',

$$\frac{P}{W} = \frac{OA'}{OB} = \frac{a}{b-c}, \text{ greatest value of } \frac{P}{W};$$

and if P be hung at B', W at A,

$$\frac{P}{W} = \frac{OA}{OB'} = \frac{a}{b+c}, \text{ least value of } \frac{P}{W}.$$

1849. (*A*). Find the relation between P and W in the system of pullies in which the same string passes round all the pullies.

(*B*). A triangular plane ABC is kept in equilibrium by three systems of pullies of the above kind, each having one block fastened to a fixed external point and the other attached to an angular point of the triangle by a string whose direction bisects the angle. The same string passes round all the pullies and is solicited by a certain force. Shew that the numbers of the strings between the pullies are as $\cos\frac{1}{2}A : \cos\frac{1}{2}B : \cos\frac{1}{2}C$.

If n be the number of the parallel strings in (*A*),

$$\frac{W}{P} = n.$$

Let n_1, n_2, n_3, be the numbers of strings between the blocks of the pullies at A, B, C, respectively. Then, by the above formula, the tensions at A, B, C, which keep the triangle at rest, will be n_1P, n_2P, n_3P; P being the force which acts upon the string passing round all the pullies. The directions of these three tensions, by hypothesis, bisect the angles of the triangle, and therefore meet in a point. Let them meet in O (fig. 43). Then, supposing O to be a point rigidly connected with the triangular plane, we may regard the tensions as acting upon it; and we have

$$n_1P : n_2P : n_3P :: \sin BOC : \sin AOC : \sin AOB,$$
$$:: \sin(\tfrac{1}{2}B + \tfrac{1}{2}C) : \sin(\tfrac{1}{2}A + \tfrac{1}{2}C) : \sin(\tfrac{1}{2}A + \tfrac{1}{2}B),$$

or $$n_1 : n_2 : n_3 :: \cos\tfrac{1}{2}A : \cos\tfrac{1}{2}B : \cos\tfrac{1}{2}C.$$

DYNAMICS.

1851. (*A*). Write down the laws of motion; giving any illustrations you please for the sake of explanation.

(*B*). If a weight of 10 lbs. be placed upon a plane which is made to descend with a uniform acceleration of 10 feet per second, what is the pressure upon the plane?

Let R be the pressure on the plane. The moving force upon the given weight

$$= 10 \text{ lbs.} - R,$$

$$= (\text{mass}) \times (\text{acceleration per second}), \text{ by the third law of motion,}$$

$$= \frac{10}{g} \, . \, 10,$$

$$= \frac{100}{32{\cdot}2} . \text{lbs.};$$

therefore $$R = 10 - \frac{100}{32{\cdot}2},$$

$$= 10 \, \frac{2{\cdot}22}{3{\cdot}22},$$

$$= 6{\cdot}895 \text{ lbs.}$$

1850. (*A*). Explain clearly on what conventions with respect to units the equation $P = Mf$ is true, where f expresses the accelerating effect of a force whose statical measure is P.

(*B*). A body weighing 10 lbs. is moved by a constant force which generates in a second a velocity of 1 foot per second; find what weight the force would support.

Here (B) is a numerical exemplification of the meaning of the equation $P = Mf$, or moving force = the product of mass into accelerating force. The question is simply this: Given the mass of body and the accelerating force, find the moving force.

Let M be mass, f accelerating force. Therefore

$$Mg = 10 \text{ lbs.} \quad \text{where } g = 32{\cdot}2 \text{ feet},$$

and $$f = 1 \text{ foot}.$$

Therefore moving force required, or in other words, the weight which it would support,

$$\begin{aligned} &= Mf, \\ &= 10 \,.\, \frac{f}{g} \text{ lbs.}, \\ &= 10 \,.\, \frac{1}{32{\cdot}2} \text{ lbs.}, \\ &= {\cdot}3105 \text{ lbs.} \end{aligned}$$

1848. (A). A body whose mass is m, is projected with a velocity V, and acted on by a constant pressure P in the line of projection: find the velocity of the body at any time.

(B). A train of connected bodies, whose weights are W_1, W_2,...... are moving together in a straight line, being acted on by the retarding pressures P_1, P_2, ... respectively; find the conditions in order that the bodies may continue to move with equal velocities when the connexion between them is severed.

In (A) we have

$$\text{velocity at time } t = V + \frac{P}{m} t.$$

Similarly, in (B), if V be the velocity of the whole train at the instant when the bodies are separated,

$$\begin{aligned} &\text{velocity of } W_1 \text{ at time } t \text{ from the separation} \\ &= V - \frac{P_1}{\text{mass of } W_1} \cdot t, \\ &= V - \frac{P_1}{W_1} \cdot gt, \end{aligned}$$

velocity of W_2 at time $t = V - \frac{P_2}{W_2} \cdot gt$,

and so on.

If then the bodies, after being severed, are to move always with the same velocities,

$$V - \frac{P_1}{W_1} \cdot gt = V - \frac{P_2}{W_2} \cdot gt = \&c....,$$

or

$$\frac{P_1}{W_1} = \frac{P_2}{W_2} = \&c....,$$

the conditions required.

1850. (*A*) Shew that in uniformly accelerated motion $s = \frac{1}{2}ft^2$.

(*B*) A body falling in vacuo, under the action of gravity, is observed to fall through 144·9 ft. and 177·1 ft. in two successive seconds; determine the accelerating force of gravity, and the time from the beginning of the motion.

Let s, s', s'' be the spaces (in feet) through which a body would fall from rest in $t-1$, t, and $t+1$ seconds respectively.

Then, by (*A*),

$$s = \tfrac{1}{2}g(t-1)^2,$$
$$s' = \tfrac{1}{2}gt^2,$$
$$s'' = \tfrac{1}{2}g(t+1)^2,$$

we have $\qquad \frac{1}{2}g(2t-1) = s' - s = 144·9 \text{ .... } (1),$

and $\qquad \frac{1}{2}g(2t+1) = s'' - s' = 177·1 \text{ .... } (2),$

from which two equations we can find g and t.

Subtracting (1) from (2),

$$g = 32.2.$$

Also

$$\frac{2t+1}{2t-1} = \frac{177·1}{144·9},$$

and therefore

$$2t = \frac{177·1 + 144·9}{177·1 - 144·9} = \frac{322}{32·2} = 10;$$

therefore

$$t = 5 \quad \text{and} \quad t + 1 = 6.$$

1849. (A). If a body be projected with a velocity u, and acted on by a uniform force f in the direction of motion, shew that the space passed over in the time t will be $ut + \frac{1}{2}ft^2$.

(B). A particle moves over 7 feet in the first second of the time during which it is observed, and over 11 and 17 feet in the third and sixth seconds respectively. Is this consistent with the supposition of its being subject to the action of a uniform force?

Let the velocity with which the particle is moving when first observed be u. Then, if it is acted on by a uniform force (f), and s be the space passed over in t'', we have, by (A),

$$s = ut + \tfrac{1}{2}ft^2.$$

Hence, space described in the first second, (s_1)

$$= u + \tfrac{1}{2}f,$$
$$= 7, \text{ by hypothesis.}$$

So $$s_3 = (3u + \tfrac{1}{2}f.3^2) - (2u + \tfrac{1}{2}f.2^2),$$
$$= u + \tfrac{5}{2}f,$$
$$= 11, \text{ by hypothesis.}$$

We now have two equations, from which we find

$$f = 2 \text{ feet},$$
$$u = 6 \text{ feet};$$

therefore $$s_6 = (6u + \tfrac{1}{2}f.6^2) - (5u + \tfrac{1}{2}f.s^2),$$
$$= u + \tfrac{11}{2}.f,$$
$$= 6 + 11,$$
$$= 17.$$

Therefore the assumption that the particle is under the action of a uniform force is consistent with the data.

1850. (A). Prove that if a heavy body fall down a smooth curve, the velocity at any point will be that due to the vertical height through which it has fallen.

(*B*). Shew how to place a plane of given length in order that a body may acquire a given velocity by falling down it.

Let a (fig. 44) be the given length of the plane, v the given velocity. Take a vertical line $AB = \frac{v^2}{2g}$. With centre A and radius $= a$, describe in a vertical plane a circle cutting the horizontal line through B in C.

AC will be the position required.

For, by (*A*),

$$\text{velocity at } C = \text{velocity due to } AB,$$
$$= \sqrt{(2g.AB)},$$
$$= v.$$

1848. (*A*). Prove that a body projected obliquely and acted on by gravity will describe a parabola.

(*B*). Find the velocity and direction of projection in order that the projectile may pass horizontally through a given point.

Since the proposition teaches us that the path of a projectile is a parabola whose axis is vertical, it is clear that the given point A (fig. 45) must be the vertex of the parabola. Let P be the point of projection; $PB = h$, $BA = k$. We may deduce from (*A*), exactly as in Goodwin's *Course* (Dynamics, Art. 39, 3rd edit.),

$$h = \frac{V^2}{2g} \cdot \sin 2\alpha,$$

$$k = \frac{V^2}{2g} \cdot \sin^2 \alpha.$$

Hence, $$\frac{k}{h} = \frac{\sin^2 \alpha}{\sin 2\alpha} = \tfrac{1}{2} \tan \alpha;$$

therefore $$\alpha = \tan^{-1} \left(\frac{2k}{h}\right),$$

and $$V^2 = \frac{2gh}{\sin 2\alpha},$$

$$= gh \cdot \frac{1 + \tan^2\alpha}{\tan \alpha},$$

$$= \frac{g}{2k} \cdot (h^2 + 4k^2).$$

1850. (*A*). Find the curve described by a body projected in vacuo with a given velocity and in a given direction, explaining the application of the second law of motion to the problem.

(*B*). A smooth tube of uniform bore is bent into the form of a circular arc greater than a semicircle, and placed in a vertical plane with its open ends upwards and in the same horizontal line. Find the velocity with which a ball that fits the tube must be projected along the interior from the lowest point, in order that it may pass out at one end and re-enter at the other.

The result of (*A*) is (see Goodwin's *Course*, p. 269, 3rd edit.) that if V (fig. 46) be the velocity of projection from P in direction PT,

$$QV^2 = \frac{2V^2}{g} \cdot PV,$$

and therefore the path is a parabola.

Let now PCP' (fig. 47) be the tube mentioned in (*B*). $OP = a$, $ON = c$, $\angle POP' = 2\alpha$,

v = velocity of projection from C,

v' = velocity with which the ball emerges from P or P'.

By (*A*) it will describe a parabola; and the given conditions shew that PT, $P'T$ are tangents to this parabola, whose vertex therefore will be at A, the middle point of NT.

Also, by (*A*), we have

$$PT^2 = \frac{2v'^2}{g} \cdot AT.$$

But
$$PT = a \,.\, \tan\alpha,$$
$$AT = \tfrac{1}{2}NT = \tfrac{1}{2}(a \,.\, \sec\alpha - c),$$
$$= \tfrac{1}{2}(a \,.\, \sec\alpha - a \,.\, \cos\alpha).$$

Therefore
$$a^2 . \tan^2\alpha = \frac{v'^2}{g} \,.\, a\,(\sec\alpha - \cos\alpha),$$

or
$$ag \,.\, \tan^2\alpha = v'^2 \frac{1 - \cos^2\alpha}{\cos\alpha};$$

therefore
$$v'^2 = ag \,.\, \sec\alpha.$$

Now the velocity at C is same as if the ball had been projected downwards with velocity v' from N; therefore
$$v^2 = v'^2 + 2g \,.\, CN,$$
$$= ag \,.\, \sec\alpha + 2g \,.\, (a + c),$$
$$= ag \,.\, (2 + 2\cos\alpha + \sec\alpha).$$

1849. (A). The velocity of a projectile at any point of its parabolic path is that which would be acquired by a body falling freely from the directrix to that point.

(B). If a body be projected with a given velocity so as to pass through a given point, construct the direction of projection.

We learn immediately from (A) that, if a body be projected with a given velocity, the distance of the point (P) of projection from the directrix is known, and consequently the position of the directrix. The body has also to pass through a given point (Q); so that (B) is equivalent to the geometrical problem: to draw through P a tangent to the parabola which passes through the given points P, Q, and whose directrix is known.

Draw PM, QN (fig. 48) perpendicular to the directrix. With centres P and Q, and with radii PM, QN respectively, describe two circles, cutting one another in S, S'. Join PS, PS', QS, QS'. Then, since $PM = PS$, $QN = QS$, and also $PM = PS'$, $QN = QS'$, it is clear that each of the points S, S' will be the focus of a parabola which answers the given conditions. Hence there are two solutions; and both the line PT bisecting the angle

SPM, and the line PT'' bisecting the angle $S'PM$, will be the direction in which the body must be projected with the given velocity so as to pass through Q.

1850. (A). Given the velocities of two bodies of which the masses are M, M', and the elasticity e; find the velocity of each body after a direct collision.

(B). Three equal balls are moving in the same direction with velocities which are proportional to 3, 2, 1; and the distances between them were at a given time the same: shew that after impact the velocities will continue to be in arithmetical progression.

(B) is not a direct application of (A), because it involves a double impact; it is rather a question of similar character, and must be solved in the same style as (A).

Let m (fig. 49) = mass of each ball; $3v$, $2v$, v, the velocities of the balls, beginning with the hindermost, before impact; v_3, v_2, v_1, velocities *after* impact.

The ratios of the velocities of the balls before impact shew that, since they are at the same distance at a given time, they will be equidistant always, and therefore will impinge on one another at the same instant.

Now observing that $2v - v$ or v is the relative velocity of A_1 and A_2 before impact, and $v_1 - v_2$ after impact, and also $3v - 2v$ or v the relative velocity of A_3, A_2 before, and $v_2 - v_3$ after impact, we get

$$v_1 - v_2 = e.v,$$

$$v_2 - v_3 = e.v;$$

which proves that v_1, v_2, v_3 are in arithmetical progression.

Had (B) been a *problem*, disjoined from any proposition, it might readily have been solved thus:

Impress on all three bodies a velocity $= -2v$; then A_2 is brought to rest, the velocities of A_3, A_1 are v and $-v$ respectively; *i.e.* they impinge (at the same moment) on A_2 at rest with *equal* velocity (v). Therefore A_2 still remains at rest, while A_3, A_1 bound back with equal velocities $-ev$, ev. Impress on the whole system the velocity $2v$. Then the velocities of A_3, A_2, A_1 are

$$2v - ev, \quad 2v, \quad \text{and } 2v + ev,$$

which are in arithmetical progression.

1849. (A). A heavy particle slides down an inclined plane of given height under the action of gravity; find the time of descent and the velocity acquired.

(B). If at the bottom of the inclined plane it rebound from a hard horizontal plane, what must be the inclination of the former that the range on the latter may be the greatest possible?

If h be the given height of the plane, V the velocity acquired at the bottom of it,

$$V^2 = 2gh.$$

Let now θ be the inclination of the plane to the horizon; e the modulus of elasticity between the particle and the horizontal plane; v the velocity with which, and θ' the angle to the horizon at which, the particle rebounds. We have

$$\text{the range on the horizontal plane} = \frac{v^2}{g} \cdot \sin 2\theta',$$

$$= \frac{V^2}{g} \cdot (\cos^2\theta + e^2 . \sin^2\theta) . \sin 2\theta'.$$

Also $$\tan\theta' = e . \tan\theta.$$

Therefore $$\sin 2\theta' = \frac{2\tan\theta'}{1 + \tan^2\theta'} = \frac{e . \sin 2\theta}{\cos^2\theta + e^2 . \sin^2\theta};$$

$$\text{therefore the range} = \frac{V^2}{g} . e . \sin 2\theta,$$

$$= 2h . e \sin 2\theta.$$

This (since h is given) will be greatest when

$$\sin 2\theta = 1, \quad \text{or } 2\theta = 90^\circ, \quad \text{or } \theta = 45^\circ.$$

1850. (*A*). If a particle oscillate in a cycloid, the time of an oscillation will be independent of the arc of vibration.

(*B*). A seconds pendulum was too long on a given day by a small quantity α; it was then over-corrected so as to be too short by α during the next day: shew that the number of minutes gained in the two days was $1080\,\frac{\alpha^2}{L^2}$ nearly, if L be the length of the seconds pendulum.

The result of the investigation in (*A*) is that

$$\text{time of oscillation} = \pi\sqrt{\frac{l}{g}},$$

where $l = 2$ diameter of generating circle,

$= $ radius of curvature at vertex of cycloid.

If a pendulum of length l make small oscillations about one extremity, we may consider the other extremity as moving very nearly in a cycloid the radius of whose generating circle is $\frac{l}{2}$; and therefore

$$\text{time of oscillation} = \pi\sqrt{\frac{l}{g}}.$$

Hence we can apply this formula to (*B*).

Since L is the length of the seconds pendulum,

$$1 = \pi\sqrt{\frac{L}{g}} \quad\text{......................}\quad (1).$$

Let t_1 be the time of an oscillation (in seconds) on the first day when the length of the pendulum is $L + \alpha$; t_2 on the second day, when the length of the pendulum is $L - \alpha$; y_1 the number of oscillations made on the first day; y_2 on the second day. N the number of seconds in a day. Then

$$t_1 = \pi\sqrt{\left(\frac{L+\alpha}{g}\right)} \quad\text{....................}\quad (2),$$

$$t_2 = \pi\sqrt{\left(\frac{L-\alpha}{g}\right)} \quad\text{....................}\quad (3),$$

$$t_1 = \frac{N}{y_1} \quad \ldots\ldots\ldots\ldots\ldots\ldots\ldots\ldots \quad (4),$$

$$t_2 = \frac{N}{y_2} \quad \ldots\ldots\ldots\ldots\ldots\ldots\ldots\ldots \quad (5),$$

and number of seconds lost or gained $= (y_1 + y_2) \sim 2N$.

Now $y_1 + y_2 = \frac{N}{t_1} + \frac{N}{t_2}$ from (4) and (5),

$$= \left\{\frac{1}{\pi}\sqrt{\left(\frac{g}{L+\alpha}\right)} + \frac{1}{\pi}\sqrt{\left(\frac{g}{L-\alpha}\right)}\right\} N, \text{ from (2) and (3),}$$

$$= \frac{1}{\pi}\sqrt{\frac{g}{L}}\left\{\left(1+\frac{\alpha}{L}\right)^{-\frac{1}{2}} + \left(1-\frac{\alpha}{L}\right)^{-\frac{1}{2}}\right\} N,$$

$$= \left\{\left(1+\frac{\alpha}{L}\right)^{-\frac{1}{2}} + \left(1-\frac{\alpha}{L}\right)^{-\frac{1}{2}}\right\} N, \text{ from (1),}$$

$$= \left\{\left(1 - \frac{1}{2}\cdot\frac{\alpha}{L} + \frac{3}{8}\cdot\frac{\alpha^2}{L^2} - \ldots\right) + \left(1 + \frac{1}{2}\cdot\frac{\alpha}{L} + \frac{3}{8}\cdot\frac{\alpha^2}{L^2} + \ldots\right)\right\} N,$$

$$= \left(2 + \frac{3}{4}\cdot\frac{\alpha^2}{L^2}\right) N, \text{ neglecting fourth \&c. powers of } \frac{\alpha}{L}.$$

Therefore number of seconds *gained*

$$= \frac{3}{4}\cdot\frac{\alpha^2}{L^2} N = \frac{3}{4}\cdot\frac{\alpha^2}{L^2}\, 24 \times 60 \times 60,$$

therefore number of minutes gained

$$= \frac{3}{4}\cdot\frac{\alpha^2}{L^2}\, 24 \times 60,$$

$$= 1080 \cdot \frac{\alpha^2}{L^2}.$$

1851. (A). If a body move from rest under the action of a uniform accelerating force, prove that the space moved over varies as the square of the time of motion.

(B). If a body fall down an inclined plane, and another be projected from the starting-point horizontally along the plane; find the distance between the two bodies when the first has descended through a given space.

Since the second body is projected horizontally along the plane, it will, by the second law of motion, be affected by the action of gravity exactly in the same degree as the first body; that is, the bodies will always be in the same horizontal line. Let then either body descend through the given space (s) in the time t; and let V be the velocity of projection of the second body.

The distance between the bodies at the time $t = Vt$. But, by (A),

$$s = \tfrac{1}{2}g.\sin\alpha.t^2,$$

α being the inclination of the plane to the horizon. Therefore

$$t = \sqrt{\left(\frac{2s}{g\sin\alpha}\right)},$$

and therefore the distance between the bodies $= V.\sqrt{\left(\frac{2s}{g\sin\alpha}\right)}$.

1851. (A). A ball impinges directly with a given velocity upon another ball at rest; find the velocity of each after impact, their common elasticity being e.

(B). If the vis viva before impact be n times the vis viva after impact, find their common elasticity.

The formulæ arrived at in the investigation of (A), (with the usual notation), are

$$v = V - (1+e).\frac{M'}{M+M'}.V,$$

$$v' = (1+e).\frac{M}{M+M'}.V.$$

From these we obtain the two following relations:

$$Mv + M'v' = MV,$$

$$v - v' = -eV.$$

Therefore $$(Mv + M'v')^2 = M^2V^2,$$

and $$MM'(v-v')^2 = MM'e^2V^2.$$

Adding,

$$(M+M')(Mv^2 + M'v'^2) = (M + e^2M').MV^2.$$

Now, by hypothesis,

$$n.(Mv^2 + M'v'^2) = MV^2.$$

Therefore $$M + M' = n.(M + e^2.M'),$$

therefore $$e = \left\{\frac{M' - (n-1).M}{nM'}\right\}^{\frac{1}{2}}.$$

1848. (*A*). If two imperfectly elastic balls, moving with given velocities in a straight line, impinge directly, find their velocities after impact.

(*B*). If the first *A*, of three perfectly elastic balls placed in a line, impinge directly with a given velocity on the second *B*, so that *B* in turn impinges on the third *C*, find the mass of *B* in order that the velocity given to *C* may be the greatest possible, the masses of *A* and *C* being known.

The formulæ investigated in (*A*) are (see Goodwin's *Dynamics*, Art. 50),

$$v = V - (1+e) \cdot \frac{M'}{M+M'} \cdot (V - V'),$$

$$v' = V' + (1+e) \cdot \frac{M'}{M+M'} \cdot (V - V').$$

Let M, M', M'' be the masses of the three bodies A, B, C; V the velocity of A before impact. Then, since B is supposed to be at rest before A impinges on it, and also, the bodies being *perfectly* elastic, $e = 1$, we have, for the velocity of B after impact,

$$v' = \frac{2M}{M+M'} \cdot V.$$

Now B impinges on C at rest with the velocity v'; hence, if v'' be the velocity of C after impact,

$$v'' = \frac{2M'}{M'+M''} \cdot v',$$

$$= \frac{4MM'}{(M+M')(M'+M'')} \cdot V.$$

We have to find what value of M' will make v'' the greatest possible, having given V, M, and M''.

v'' will be the greatest when $\frac{(M+M')(M'+M'')}{M'}$ is least;

$$i.e.\text{ when}\qquad M+M''+M'+\frac{MM''}{M'}\text{ is least,}$$

$$\text{or when}\qquad M'+\frac{MM''}{M'}\text{ is least.}$$

Let this quantity $= u$. Therefore

$$M'^2 - u.M' + MM'' = 0.$$

$$\text{Whence}\qquad M' = \tfrac{1}{2}u \pm \tfrac{1}{2}\surd(u^2 - 4MM''),$$

from which we see that the least value which u can possibly take is given by $u^2 = 4MM''$; and we then have

$$M' = \tfrac{1}{2}u = \surd(MM'').$$

1849. (A). How may a pendulum be made to oscillate in a cycloid?

(B). A pendulum which oscillates seconds at one place is carried to a place where it gains two minutes a-day; compare the force of gravity at the latter place with that at the former.

When a body oscillates in a cycloid, the time of an oscillation is $\pi\sqrt{\frac{l}{g}}$, l being the length of the pendulum.

If the pendulum oscillates seconds at a place where the force of gravity is g,

$$1 = \pi\sqrt{\frac{l}{g}}.$$

If at a place where the force of gravity is g' it gains two minutes, the time of an oscillation will be $\frac{N}{N+120}$, N being the number of seconds in a day.

Therefore $$\frac{N}{N+120} = \pi\sqrt{\frac{l}{g'}}.$$

Hence $$\frac{g'}{g} = \left(\frac{N+120}{N}\right)^2,$$

$$= \left(1 + \frac{1}{720}\right)^2.$$

1851. (*A*). Define a cycloid, and prove that the arc measured from the vertex to any point is equal to twice that chord of the generating circle which touches the curve at that point.

(*B*). Hence deduce the radius of curvature at the vertex, and shew that the time of oscillation in a small arc of the generating circle will be half the time of oscillation in the cycloid.

The radius of curvature at C, (fig. 50),

$$= \tfrac{1}{2} \text{ limit } \frac{CP^2}{Pn},$$

$$= \tfrac{1}{2} \text{ limit } \frac{(2PR)^2}{Pn}, \text{ by } (A),$$

$$= 2 \text{ limit } \frac{pC^2}{pn},$$

$$= 2CB.$$

Again, by means of the property enunciated in (*A*), it is proved that the time of oscillation in the cycloid

$$= \pi\sqrt{\left(\frac{2CB}{g}\right)},$$

$$= \pi\sqrt{\left(\frac{\text{radius of curvature at } C}{g}\right)}.$$

Hence, the time of a small oscillation in the generating circle CpB, which is the same as the time of oscillation in a cycloid of which CpB is the circle of curvature, is

$$\pi\sqrt{\left(\frac{\frac{1}{2}CB}{g}\right)},$$

$$= \tfrac{1}{2}\pi\sqrt{\left(\frac{2\,CB}{g}\right)},$$

$= \frac{1}{2}$ time of oscillation in the original cycloid.

HYDROSTATICS.

1850. (A). Find the pressure referred to a unit of area at any depth below the surface of a heavy incompressible fluid.

(B). If from every point in the vertical side of a rectangular vessel containing fluid a horizontal line be drawn proportional to the pressure at that point; find the locus of the extremities of such lines; and thence deduce the amount of the whole pressure upon one of the vertical sides of a cube filled with fluid, and the point of application of the resultant of the pressures.

We obtain from (A) that

$$\text{pressure at any point of a fluid} = \sigma z,$$

where σ = specific gravity of fluid, z = depth of the point below the surface.

Let $ABCD$ (fig. 51) be a vertical section of the rectangular vessel.

If from a point P in AB, a line PQ be drawn proportional to the pressure at P, PQ must, by the proposition, be proportional to AP. Therefore

$$\frac{PQ}{AP} (= \tan PAQ) \text{ is constant;}$$

and therefore the locus of Q is the straight line AQ; and therefore the locus required is a plane making a constant angle QAD with the surface of the fluid.

Let now the vessel be a cube of which $AB = a$ is one vertical edge.

Since σ is a numerical quantity, we may take

$$PQ = \sigma AP,$$

in which case PQ will represent the pressure at P. Hence the whole pressure on the line AB is equal to the sum of all the lines similar to PQ which lie between A and BR, *i.e.* = *area* ABR. Therefore whole pressure on a vertical side of the cube

$$= \textit{volume} \text{ of the solid of which } ABR \text{ is a vertical section},$$
$$= \tfrac{1}{2} \text{volume of rectangular box } ABRL,$$
$$= \tfrac{1}{2} AB^2 . BR,$$
$$= \tfrac{1}{2} a^2 . \sigma a,$$
$$= \tfrac{1}{2} \sigma a^3 .$$

Again, to determine the point of application of the fluid pressures on AB is nothing more than to determine the point of application of a system of parallel forces proportional to lines such as PQ; which problem is exactly the same as that of finding in which of the lines parallel to BR, of which the triangle ABR is made up, *the centre of gravity of the triangle* ABR lies. We know that it lies in that line which is at a distance $\frac{2}{3}AB$ from A; the point therefore (in the vertical line bisecting the side of the cube) which is at a distance $\frac{2}{3}a$ below the surface of the fluid, is the point of application of the resultant of the fluid pressures upon the side.

1849. (A). Determine the whole pressure on a surface immersed in a heavy fluid of uniform density.

(B). What must be the vertical angle of a conical vessel, in order that when it is placed with its vertex upwards, and filled with heavy fluid through a hole at the vertex, the pressure on the curved surface may be to the pressure on the base as 4 to 3?

Prove that the ratio above mentioned cannot for any cone be less than 2 : 3.

The whole pressure on a surface whose area is S, which is immersed in a fluid of specific gravity σ, and whose centre of gravity is at depth $\bar{z}$ below the surface of the fluid, is

$$\sigma \bar{z} S.$$

If h, c, r are respectively the height of the cone in (B), the length of the slant side, and the radius of the base,

$$\text{area of curved surface} = \pi rc,$$

$$\text{and depth of its centre of gravity} = \tfrac{2}{3}h;$$

therefore whole pressure on curved surface $(P_1) = \frac{2}{3}\sigma.\pi rch$.

Again, $\qquad$ area of base $= \pi r^2$,

$$\text{and depth of its centre of gravity} = h,$$

therefore whole pressure on the base $(P_2) = \sigma\pi r^2 h$.

Therefore $$\frac{2}{3}\frac{c}{r} = \frac{P_1}{P_2} = \frac{4}{3}, \text{ by hypothesis,}$$

therefore $$\frac{r}{c} = \frac{1}{2}.$$

But if θ be the semi-vertical angle of the cone,

$$\frac{r}{c} = \sin\theta.$$

therefore $$\sin\theta = \tfrac{1}{2},$$

or $$\theta = 30^\circ;$$

and therefore the vertical angle $= 60^\circ$.

Since the ratio $\frac{P_1}{P_2} = \frac{2}{3}\frac{c}{r}$; and since for no cone can c be less than r, it appears that $\frac{P_1}{P_2}$ can never be less than $\frac{2}{3}$.

1849. (A). Determine the conditions of equilibrium of a floating body.

(B). A cylindrical vessel, the radius of the base of which is one foot, contains water: if a cubic foot of cork (sp. gr. = ·24) be allowed to float in the water, find the additional pressure sustained by the curved surface, and by the base, respectively.

That a body may float, its weight must be equal to the weight of the fluid displaced, and the centres of gravity of the body and of the fluid displaced must lie in the same vertical line.

The latter condition shews that the cubic foot of cork mentioned in (B) will float in *stable* equilibrium with a side horizontal; and then the former condition gives us (if x is the depth to which the cork will sink, expressed as a fraction of a foot),

$$(\text{sp. gr. of water}) \times (1 \text{ sq. ft.}) \,.\, x = (\text{sp. gr. of cork}) \,.\, (1 \text{ cub. ft.}),$$

or $$x = \cdot 24.$$

Again, if y be the height through which the water rises when the cork is put in, the fact that the volume of the water remains the same gives

$$y\,(\text{area of base of cylinder}) = \text{volume of cork immersed},$$

or $$y.\pi = \cdot 24 \; (\because \text{radius of the base of the cylinder} = 1),$$

$$\therefore \quad y = \frac{\cdot 24}{\pi}.$$

Now the increased pressure on the curved surface will clearly be equal to the pressure on a strip of the cylinder of length y supposed added on to the *bottom* of the cylinder; *i.e.* (if h is the original height of the water)

$$= 2\pi.y.\,(h + \tfrac{1}{2}y), \text{ sp. gr. of water being } 1,$$

$$= \cdot 24\left(2h + \frac{\cdot 24}{\pi}\right).$$

The increase of pressure on the base

$$= \pi.(h + y) - \pi.h,$$

$$= \pi y,$$

$$= \cdot 24.$$

Obs. These numerical results give the ratios of the pressures to the weight of a unit of volume of water.

1849. (*A*). Define specific gravity.

(*B*). The specific gravity of coal is about 1·12, that of water being 1, and a cubic foot of water weighs 1000 oz.; find the edge of a cubical block of coal which weighs 2000 tons.

The specific gravity of a substance is the ratio of the weight of any portion of its volume to that of an equal volume of some standard substance whose specific gravity is taken as unity. Hence, water being taken as the standard substance,

$$1{\cdot}12 = \frac{\text{specific gravity of coal}}{\text{.................... water}},$$

$$= \frac{\text{weight of a cubic foot of coal}}{\text{............................ water}};$$

therefore weight of a cubic foot of coal $= 1{\cdot}12 \times 1000$ oz.

$= 1120$ oz.

$= \frac{1}{32}$ ton;

therefore weight of 2000×32 cubic feet of coal $= 2000$ tons.

Thus the volume of the block of coal is 64000 cubic feet, and the edge is therefore 40 feet.

1850. (*A*). Define specific gravity. Given weights of substances of known specific gravity are compounded; find the specific gravity of the compound.

(*B*). Eleven ounces of gold (sp. gr. 19.3) are mixed with one ounce of copper (sp. gr. 8.8), find the specific gravity of the compound, supposing its volume to be the sum of the volumes of the two metals.

The result of the investigation in (*A*) is

$$\text{sp. gr. of compound} = \sigma\sigma' . \frac{W + W'}{\sigma W' + \sigma' W},$$

assuming that the volume of the compound is the sum of the volumes of the components.

In (B), $\sigma = 19{\cdot}3$, $\sigma' = 8{\cdot}8$, $W = 11$ oz., $W' = 1$ oz.
Therefore specific gravity of compound

$$= (19.3) \, . \, (8.8) \, . \, \frac{11 + 1}{19.3 \times 1 + 8.8 \times 11},$$

$$= (19.3) \, . \, (8.8) \, . \, \frac{12}{116.1},$$

$$= (19.3) \, . \, (8.8) \, . \, \frac{4}{38.7},$$

$$= \frac{679.36}{38.7},$$

$$= 17.5054.$$

1848. (A). Describe the experiment which shews that the pressure of air is proportional to its density while the temperature remains constant.

(B). A straight vertical tube is closed at its lower end; how much of a given liquid can be poured into it, the air which originally filled it being compressed at the bottom of the tube?

Let a be the length of the tube, x the length of that portion which is filled with fluid (specific gravity σ), Π the pressure of the atmosphere, P the pressure of the air when compressed in the tube.

Since by (A) the pressure of air varies as its density, and therefore inversely as the volume it occupies,

$$\frac{P}{\Pi} = \frac{a}{a - x}.$$

But P supports the weight of a column of fluid whose height is x, together with the pressure Π on the surface of the fluid; therefore

$$P = \sigma . x + \Pi,$$

$$= \sigma \, (x + h),$$

if h is the height of a column of fluid whose weight is equal to the pressure of the atmosphere.

Therefore $$\frac{x+h}{h} = \frac{P}{\Pi} = \frac{a}{a-x},$$

therefore $$(a-h)\,x - x^2 = 0,$$

and $$x = a - h,$$

gives the length of the column of fluid in the tube.

1850. (*A*). Give the experiment from which it is inferred that the pressure of air at a given temperature varies inversely as the space it occupies.

If the temperature vary, what relation exists between the pressure, the volume, and the temperature?

(*B*). A given quantity of air under the pressure of m pounds to the square inch, occupies n cubic inches when the temperature is t; find how many cubic inches it will occupy under the pressure of m' pounds to the square inch when the temperature is t'.

The answer to the second part of (*A*) is

$$\Pi = \beta\,\frac{1+\alpha t}{v},$$ where t is temperature and v volume.

The first condition in (*B*) gives $\Pi = m$ lbs., $v = n$ cubic inches, corresponding to temperature t. Therefore

$$m = \beta\,\frac{1+\alpha t}{n} \qquad \text{.......................(1).}$$

The second condition gives $\Pi = m'$ lbs., $v = x$ cubic inches, the required volume for temperature t'. Therefore

$$m' = \beta\,\frac{1+\alpha t'}{x} \qquad \text{.......................(2).}$$

Eliminating β, $$\frac{m}{m'} = \frac{x}{n}\,\frac{1+\alpha t}{1+\alpha t'},$$

therefore $$x = n\,\frac{m}{m'}\,\frac{1+\alpha t'}{1+\alpha t},$$

where α is the expansion of a cubic inch of air for 1° of increase of temperature.

1850. (*A*). Shew how to graduate a thermometer, and to compare the scales of two differently graduated thermometers.

(*B*). The number which expresses a certain temperature on the centigrade scale is equal to the sum of the numbers which express the same temperature on Fahrenheit's and Reaumur's respectively; find the numbers.

From (*A*) we have, if a, a', be the graduations of the boiling point; b, b', of freezing point; and x, x', of any given temperature in the two thermometers,

$$\frac{x-b}{a-b} = \frac{x'-b'}{a'-b'}.$$

In the centigrade scale $a = 100$, $b = 0$.

In Fahrenheit's $a = 212$, $b = 32$.

In Reaumur's $a = 80$, $b = 0$.

Therefore x, x', x'', being numbers which represent a certain temperature in the three scales respectively,

$$\frac{x}{100} = \frac{x'-32}{180} = \frac{x''}{80},$$

or

$$\frac{x}{5} = \frac{x'-32}{9} = \frac{x''}{4}.$$

Also, by hypothesis, $x = x' + x''$.

From these three equations we have to determine x, x', x''.

We have $x = \frac{9}{5}x + 32 + \frac{4}{5}x$,

or $-\frac{8}{5}x = 32$.

Therefore $x = -20°$ Centigrade.

Therefore $x' = \frac{9}{5}x + 32$,

$= -36 + 32$,

$= -4°$ Fahrenheit.

$x'' = \frac{4}{5}x$,

$= -16°$ Reaumur.

1851. (A). Describe the Common Barometer.

(B). If there be a small quantity of air in the tube above the column of mercury, what will be the effect on the indications of the barometer?

(C). A faulty barometer indicated 29·2 and 30 inches when the indications of a correct instrument were 29·4 and 30·3 respectively, find the length of tube which the air in the tube would fill under the pressure of 30 inches.

Let h, x, be respectively the true and false readings of the barometer; c the length of tube occupied by a small quantity of air in the upper part of the tube when under the pressure indicated by the reading (h); a the whole height of the tube above the lower surface of the mercury; σ the density of the mercury. Then

pressure of external air = wt. of column of mercury of height x
+ pressure of air in upper part of the tube,

or $$\sigma h = \sigma x + \sigma h \, . \, \frac{c}{a - x},$$

therefore $$h(a - x) = x(a - x) + hc.$$

Whence $$h = \frac{x(a - x)}{a - c - x},$$

which gives the *true* reading.

The error produced $= h - x$,

$$= \frac{cx}{a - c - x}.$$

In (C) we have to apply this result to a numerical example.

When the faulty barometer indicates 29·2 ($= x$), we have by the true one, $h = 29·4$ inches; and therefore the error produced is ·2 inches. Also let $c = c_1$; therefore

$$·2 = \frac{c_1 . 29·2}{a - c_1 - 29·2};$$

therefore $$a - c_1 - 29·2 = 146 c_1,$$

therefore $$a - 29·2 = 147 c_1 \quad \text{.......................} \quad (1).$$

Again, when the faulty barometer indicates 30 inches, the error is ·3, and $c = c_2$, suppose;

therefore $$\cdot 3 = \frac{c_2 . 30}{a - c_2 - 30},$$

therefore $$a - 30 = 101c_2 \text{ ....(2)}.$$

Eliminating a from (1) and (2),

$$147c_1 - 101c_2 = \cdot 8.$$

Also, since the mass of air in the tube is the same, the volumes it successively occupies are proportional to the pressures;

therefore $$\frac{c_1}{c_2} = \frac{30.3}{29.4} = \frac{101}{98}.$$

Hence $$3.\frac{101}{2} c_2 - 101c_2 = \cdot 8,$$

$$101c_2 = 1\cdot 6,$$

or $$c_2 = \frac{1\cdot 6}{101}.$$

Let c' be the length of tube which the air in the tube would fill under the pressure of 30 inches, so that

$$\frac{c'}{c_2} = \frac{30\cdot 3}{30} = 1\cdot 01;$$

therefore $$c' = 1\cdot 01 . \frac{1\cdot 6}{101}$$

$$= \cdot 016 \text{ of an inch.}$$

1850. (*A*). Describe Nicholson's Hydrometer.

(*B*). Given two weights which cause the instrument to sink to a certain depth in two fluids, find the weight which will make it sink to the same depth in a mixture of known volumes of the two fluids.

Let w = weight of the instrument,

v = volume of fluid displaced,

W_1, W_2 the weights which sink the hydrometer in two fluids whose specific gravities are σ_1, σ_2 respectively.

Then
$$w + W_1 = \sigma_1 v \text{.......................} (1),$$
$$w + W_2 = \sigma_2 v \text{.......................} (2).$$

Let now W be the weight necessary to sink the instrument to the same depth, in a fluid compounded of volumes V_1, V_2 of the above fluids. Then, observing that the specific gravity of the mixture will be $\dfrac{\sigma_1 V_1 + \sigma_2 V_2}{V_1 + V_2}$,
$$w + W = \frac{\sigma_1 V_1 + \sigma_2 V_2}{V_1 + V_2} . v \text{..............} (3);$$

therefore
$$W - W_1 = \left(\frac{\sigma_1 V_1 + \sigma_2 V_2}{V_1 + V_2} - \sigma_1\right) . v$$
$$= \frac{(\sigma_2 - \sigma_1) . V_2}{V_1 + V_2} . v.$$

Also, from (1) and (2),
$$(\sigma_2 - \sigma_1)\, v = W_2 - W_1;$$

therefore
$$W = W_1 + \frac{V_2}{V_1 + V_2} . (W_2 - W_1)$$
$$= \frac{V_1 W_1 + V_2 W_2}{V_1 + V_2}.$$

1849. (A). Describe Smeaton's Air-pump, and find the density of air in the receiver after any number of ascents of the piston.

(B). If instead of the receiver we use a cylindrical vessel of ten times the capacity of the barrel, and cover the upper extremity with a diaphragm capable of sustaining only half the pressure of the atmosphere, find after how many ascents of the piston the diaphragm will burst. Given
$$\log_{10} 2 = 0.3010300,$$
$$\log_{10} 11 = 1.0413927.$$

Generally, if A, B be the capacities of the receiver and barrel respectively, ρ the density of atmospheric air, ρ_n the density of air in the pump after n ascents of the piston,

$$\rho_n = \rho \cdot \left(\frac{A}{A+B}\right)^n.$$

Here $A = 10B$; and if n is the number of ascents of the piston just before the diaphragm bursts, $\rho_n = \frac{1}{2}\rho$, since it is only capable of sustaining half the pressure of the atmosphere;

therefore $$\tfrac{1}{2} = \left(\frac{10}{11}\right)^n;$$

therefore $$n\,(\log_{10} 11 - \log_{10} 10) = \log_{10} 2,$$

or $$n = \frac{\log_{10} 2}{\log_{10} 11 - 1}$$

$$= \frac{\cdot 3010300}{\cdot 0413927}$$

$$= 7{\cdot}2\ldots$$

Hence the diaphragm will burst during the 8th ascent.

OPTICS.

1849. (*A*). When rays diverging from a point are incident on a plane mirror, prove that the reflected rays diverge accurately from a point.

(*B*). Within what space must the eye be situated to see a given point by reflection at the mirror; and within what space must a point be situated to be seen by the eye in a given position?

Let AB be the mirror; P (fig. 52) a given point. Its image will by (*A*), be a fixed point p equally distant from the mirror on the opposite side. Join BA, pB, and produce these lines to Q, R. Then will QpR be the reflected pencil, and consequently $QABR$ the space within which an eye must be situated in order to see p.

Again, let E (fig. 53) be the eye in a given position. Draw the lines EAq, EBr. Then the image of the point must lie in the space $qABr$; and therefore, drawing AQ, BR at the same inclination to AB as Aq, Br respectively, the point, in order to be seen by the eye at E, must lie within the space $QABR$.

1851. (*A*). A luminous point is placed between two parallel plane mirrors, find the position of the successive images.

(*B*). When the luminous point moves uniformly in a straight line, shew that all the images will move uniformly in two sets of parallel straight lines which are equally inclined to the mirrors.

Let Q (fig. 54) be the luminous point. Then if we consider the rays which fall first upon the mirror A, an image Q_1 is formed, then an image Q_2 of Q_1 by the mirror B, then an image Q_3 of Q_2 by the mirror A, and so on. And a similar set of images will be formed by the rays which fall first on the mirror B.

Now if Q move along a line QP_1, Q_1 will by the nature of reflection move along Q_1P_1. Let Q_1P_1 produced meet the mirror B in P_2; then Q_2 will move along Q_2P_2. So Q_3 will move along Q_3P_3; and so on.

Thus the alternate images will move along two sets of lines respectively parallel to Q_1P_1, QP_1; lines which are equally inclined to either mirror.

It is clear that the same holds also for the images formed by rays falling first upon the mirror B.

1851. (A). Two rays are incident at any point of a spherical mirror whose centre is E, the one parallel to the axis of the mirror, the other proceeding from a point Q in the axis, and the reflected rays cut the axis in G and q respectively; shew that $GQ.Gq = GE^2$.

(B). If the axis AE of the spherical mirror meet the surface produced in R, shew that a ray proceeding from R and making an angle of 30° with the axis, will be reflected to the principal focus of the mirror.

Let the ray RP (fig. 55) incident at P make an angle of 30° with RA. Join PA; and let Pq be the reflected ray.

It is clear that the triangle APE is equiangular and therefore equilateral. Hence a ray incident at P parallel to RA will be reflected in PA. Applying therefore the formula of (A),

$$Aq.AR = AE^2 = AP^2;$$

which shews that Pq is perpendicular to Aq;

and therefore $$Aq = qE;$$

or q is the principal focus.

1851. (A). If parallel rays be incident directly upon a spherical refracting surface, the distance of the geometrical focus of refracted rays from the surface is to its distance from the centre as the index of refraction to unity.

(B). A pencil of parallel rays is incident directly upon a spherical refracting surface, and after refraction converges to a point at a distance from the surface equal to three times the radius; find the index of refraction, (1) when the surface is concave, (2) when it is convex.

By (A), if O (figs. 56, 57) be the centre of the refractor, F the geometrical focus of rays parallel to the axis,

$$AF : OF :: \mu : 1.$$

In (B), $$AF = 3\,OA,$$

and, whether the refractor be concave or convex,

$$OF = AF - OA = 2\,OA;$$

therefore, in both cases,

$$\mu = \frac{AF}{OF} = \tfrac{3}{2}.$$

1849. (A). When divergent rays are incident nearly perpendicularly upon a spherical refracting surface, the distance of the focus of incident rays from the principal focus of rays coming in a contrary direction, is to its distance from the centre of the refractor as its distance from the surface to its distance from the geometrical focus of refracted rays.

(B). If the conjugate foci are each at a distance from the surface equal to twice the radius, what is the index of refraction?

In (B), since the conjugate foci (Q, q) (fig. 58) are on opposite sides of the surface, the refractor is convex. Let O be its centre, F the principal focus of rays coming in a contrary direction.

By (A), $$QF : QO :: QA : Qq.$$

But by hypothesis, $$AQ = Aq = 2\,OA;$$

therefore $$QO = 3\,OA, \quad Qq = 2\,QA.$$

Hence, substituting $$QF : 3\,OA :: 1 : 2,$$

or $$QF = \tfrac{3}{2}\,OA;$$

therefore $$AF = AQ - QF = \tfrac{1}{2}\,OA,$$

and $$OF = OA + AF = \tfrac{3}{2}\,OA.$$

But $$AF : OF :: \mu : 1,$$

(Goodwin's *Course*, *Optics*, Art. 39, 3rd edit.)

therefore $$\mu = \frac{AF}{OF}$$ $$= \tfrac{1}{3}.$$

1848. (A). The image of a straight line formed by a plane refracting surface is a straight line. Why does a straight rod appear bent when partly immersed in water?

(B). What must be its inclination to the horizon when its apparent portions are inclined to each other at the greatest angle?

Let ABQ (fig. 59) be a rod partly immersed in water, Q any point of the rod under water, qBa the direction after refraction of the ray from Q which falls in the direction QB. Then to a first approximation, q will be the image of Q, and qB will be, by (A), the apparent position of the portion BQ of the rod.

Now the angle between the apparent portions of the rod, viz. the $\angle QBq$, is also the deviation of the ray QB. But the deviation increases as the angle of incidence increases; the angle therefore between the apparent portions of the rod will be greatest when the angle of incidence of the ray QB is greatest, *i.e.* when it equals the *critical angle* for water $= 48°\ 30'$, or when the inclination of the rod to the horizon is $41°\ 30'$.

1850. (A). Point out the distinction between a real and virtual image.

(B). A plane mirror is placed perpendicular to the axis of a concave spherical reflector, nearer to the principal focus than to the face, and between them; rays from a very distant object fall directly upon the spherical mirror: trace the pencil by which an eye will see the image formed after two reflexions at each mirror.

Let O (fig. 60) be the centre of the spherical mirror, F the principal focus half-way between O and the mirror, aCb the plane mirror, CF being less than CA, E the position of the eye.

Take $Cq = CF$; then q_1 will lie on the right of the mirror. The focus conjugate to q_1 will be at a point q_2, such that

$$-\frac{1}{Aq_2}+\frac{1}{Aq_1}=\frac{2}{AO}.$$

Again, take $Cq_3 = Cq_2$; join Eq_3, meeting the plane mirror in R_1, – R_1q_2, meeting the spherical mirror in R_2, – R_2q, meeting, when produced, ab in R_3, – FR_3, meeting, when produced, the spherical mirror in R_4; and lastly, draw R_4Q parallel to AO.

Then will $QR_4R_3R_2R_1E$ be clearly the course of the axis of the pencil by which the eye at E sees the distant object after two reflexions at each of the mirrors.

The image seen will be at q_3, which, since the rays do not actually pass through it, is a *virtual* one.

1850. (A). A ray of light is refracted through a prism in a plane perpendicular to its edge; find the deviation produced by the refraction.

(B). A speck is situated just within a glass sphere; shew how much of the surface of the sphere must be covered in order that the speck may be invisible at all points outside the sphere on a line drawn from the speck through the centre.

If ϕ, ψ, be the angles of incidence and emergence of a ray which passes through a cone whose vertical angle is i, the deviation $= \phi + \psi - i$.

Let now A (fig. 61) be a speck just within a glass sphere ADB. Let AD be a ray which, after refraction, is parallel to BC; this will clearly be the ray which makes the greatest angle with AB of all those which enter an eye situated in BC. Draw the two tangent planes to the sphere at D and A, meeting in E. Then, (since it is immaterial whether we consider it as just inside or just outside the surface,) ADF may be regarded as the course of a ray refracted through the prism AED; and our object is to find how this prism must be situated in order that the emergent ray may be parallel to BC.

We have $$\phi = \angle OAD.$$

In order that the emergent ray may be parallel to BC, the deviation must $= \angle DAO = \phi$;

therefore $$\phi = \phi + \psi - i,$$

or $$\psi = i.$$

Also $$2\phi = \angle DOB = i = \psi;$$

therefore $$\sin\psi = \mu . \sin\phi$$
$$= \mu . \sin\tfrac{1}{2}\psi;$$

or $$2\cos\tfrac{1}{2}\psi = \mu,$$

therefore $$\psi = 2\cos^{-1}\tfrac{1}{2}\mu$$
$$= \angle DOB.$$

Hence the portion of the sphere which must be covered is that which subtends an angle $DOD' = 2\angle DOB = 4\cos^{-1}\tfrac{1}{2}\mu$.

1851. (A). Shew how to find by experiment the focal length of a lens.

(B). The least distance between an object and its image formed by a plano-convex lens of glass is 12 inches; the index of refraction being $\frac{3}{2}$, find the radius of the spherical surface.

The focal length of a convex lens may be found experimentally by observing the least distance between an object in the axis of the lens and its image formed by the lens. For let Q (fig. 62) be the object, q its image, $AQ = u$, $Aq = v$, f focal length of lens.

Then $$\frac{1}{v} - \frac{1}{u} = -\frac{1}{f};$$

therefore $$Qq = -v + u$$

$$= \frac{fu}{u-f} + u$$

$$= \frac{u^2}{u-f}$$

$$= x, \text{ suppose};$$

therefore $$u^2 - xu = -fx,$$

or $$u = \tfrac{1}{2}x \pm \sqrt{\{\tfrac{1}{4}x(x-4f)\}},$$

which shews (since u must be a possible quantity) that the least value of $x = 4f$.

Thus $f = \frac{1}{4}$ of least distance between Q and its image. If the lens be concave, the focal length may be determined by the same experiment, by placing it in contact with a convex lens. (See Griffin's *Optics*, 2nd edit., Art. 167).

In (B) we have given that the least distance between an object and its image is 12 inches;

therefore $$f = \tfrac{12}{4} = 3 \text{ inches}.$$

But if r be the radius of the curved surface,

$$\frac{1}{f} = (\mu - 1) \cdot \frac{1}{r}, \text{ disregarding the sign,}$$

$$= (\tfrac{3}{2} - 1) \cdot \frac{1}{r}$$

$$= \frac{1}{2r};$$

therefore $$r = \tfrac{1}{2}f$$

$$= \tfrac{3}{2} \text{ in.}$$

1848. (*A*). Describe the Astronomical Telescope; trace the course of a pencil of rays from any point of a distant object, and find the magnifying power.

(*B*). If the focal lengths of the lenses be 12 inches and 1 inch, how far must the eye-glass be moved for viewing an object at a distance of 40 feet from the object-glass?

Let A, a (fig. 63) be the object and eye glasses of an Astronomical Telescope, p the image of an object 40 feet distant from A.

Then, since A is a convex lens of 12 inches focal length,

$$\frac{1}{Ap} - \frac{1}{480} = -\frac{1}{12};$$

therefore $$\frac{1}{Ap} = -\frac{13}{160};$$

therefore $$Ap = -\frac{160}{13} \text{ in.}$$

$$= -\left(12 + \frac{4}{13}\right) \text{ in.}$$

And since $ap = 1$ inch; therefore $Aa = 13 + \frac{4}{13}$ inches.

Now when the instrument is in adjustment for viewing a *distant* object, $Aa = 13$ inches. Hence the eye-glass has to be pulled out $\frac{4}{13}$ of an inch.

NEWTON.

1850. (A). Enunciate and prove Newton's second Lemma.

(B). Hence shew that two quantities may vanish in an infinite ratio to each other.

Taking the figure as constructed in the Lemma, we have it proved by the Lemma that the sum of the parallelograms ab, bc, cd,* &c. vanishes in the limit; and *à fortiori* the parallelogram ab vanishes. But in the limit the number of these parallelograms is infinite, and therefore the above-mentioned sum is infinitely greater than the parallelogram ab. Hence two quantities may vanish in an infinite ratio to each other.

1849. (A). Enunciate and prove Newton's fourth Lemma.

(B). In Lemma x., if the velocity vary as the square of the time, shew that the space will vary as the cube of the time.

In Lemma x. the time is divided into equal intervals represented by the lines AB, BC, CD, ... (fig. 64); the velocities being represented by lines perpendicular to these, Bb, Cc, Dd.

It is hence shewn that if Ak be the curve passing through all the points b, c, d, &c., when brought indefinitely near to one another,

space in time AD : space in time AK :: area ADd : area AKk.

Let the time AK be divided into the same number of equal parts as AD is divided into.

Then, since the velocity varies as the square of the time in which it is generated, the parallelogram Ab is proportional to AB^3, Bc to $BC.AC^2$ or $2^2.AB^3$, CD to 3^2AB^3; and

* See the figure in Goodwin's *Newton*, Lemma II.

so on. Similarly, if AB', $B'C'$, &c. are the intervals into which AK is divided, Ab' will be proportional to AB'^3, $B'c'$ to $2^2.AB'^3$, $C'd'$ to $3^2.AB'^3$, and so on. Thus the ratio of each one of the former series of parallelograms to the corresponding one of the latter series is $AB^3 : AB'^3$, or (since the number of intervals in AD, AK is the same), $AD^3 : AK^3$.

But by Lemma IV. the curvilinear areas ADd, AKk will be in the same ratio.

Therefore, from above,

$$\text{space in time } AD : \text{space in time } AK :: AD^3 : AK^3,$$

or the spaces are proportional to the cubes of the times.

1851. (A). Enunciate and prove Newton's fourth Lemma.

(B). Apply this Lemma to prove that the area included between a hyperbola and the tangents at the vertices of the conjugate hyperbola is equal to the area included between the conjugate hyperbola and the tangents at the vertices of the hyperbola.

Let the semiaxes CA, CB, (fig. 65) of the hyperbola be divided each into the same number (n) of small equal parts.

Let mm' be the $(r+1)^{\text{th}}$ part of CB, counting from C; so that

$$mm' = \frac{BC}{n}, \quad \text{and} \quad PN = Cm = \frac{r}{n}.BC.$$

Now $$CN^2 - AC^2 = AN.NM = \frac{AC^2}{BC^2}.PN^2$$
$$= \frac{r^2}{n^2}.AC^2;$$

therefore $$CN = AC.\sqrt{\left(1+\frac{r^2}{n^2}\right)}.$$

Hence the area of the small parallelogram in P is

$$mm'.mP$$
$$= \frac{BC}{n}.CN$$
$$= \frac{BC.AC}{n}.\sqrt{\left(1+\frac{r^2}{n^2}\right)}.$$

Now the conjugate hyperbola is a concentric hyperbola having AM for its transverse axis. Hence, if we divide $BCAK$ into n parallelograms of equal breadth parallel to BC, we shall find the area of the $(r+1)^{\text{th}}$ parallelogram from C

$$= \frac{AC.BC}{n} \cdot \sqrt{\left(1 + \frac{r^2}{n^2}\right)},$$

by the formula already proved.

We therefore have

$$\frac{\text{area of } Pm'}{\text{area of corresponding parallelogram in fig. } CK} = 1.$$

Thus we have divided the figs. $BCAK$, $BCAL$ into the same number of parallelograms, each of which in one figure has ultimately to the corresponding one in the other a ratio of equality. Hence, by the Lemma, the figures themselves have to one another a ratio of equality; and therefore the figures KK', LL', which are four times the former figures, are equal to one another.

1849. (A). Define similar curves.

(B). Shew that all parabolas are similar to each other.

(C). Describe an instrument which is adapted for drawing curves similar to given curves.

Two curves are said to be similar, when there can be drawn in them two distances from two points similarly situated, such that if any two other distances be drawn equally inclined to the former, the four are proportional. (Evans's Newton, Cor. to Lem. v.)

Let P (fig. 66) be any point in a parabola. Draw the tangent PT and the perpendicular PY upon it from the focus.

By the property of the parabola,

$$SY^2 = SA.SP;$$

therefore
$$\frac{SP}{SA} = \frac{SY^2}{SA^2}.$$

Let A', S', Y', be points in any other parabola corresponding to A, S, Y; P' a point in this new parabola, such that

$$\angle A'S'P' = \angle ASP.$$

Then, as above, $$\frac{S'P'}{S'A'} = \frac{S'Y'^2}{S'A'^2}.$$

Now since the $\angle A'S'P' = \angle ASP$, therefore the $\angle A'S'Y' = \angle ASY$. Hence the triangles $A'S'Y'$, ASY are similar, and therefore

$$\frac{S'Y'}{S'A'} = \frac{SY}{SA};$$

therefore $$\frac{S'P'}{S'A'} = \frac{SP}{SA},$$

which, in accordance with the above definition, proves the parabolas to be similar.

Again, let it be required to draw a curve similar to a given curve APB.

Let BC, bc (fig. 67) be two equal parallel rulers joined together by two equal parallel rulers Bb, Cc on hinges at B, b, C, c. APp a rod moveable about a hinge at A.

If now we suppose BC, bc, and APp to have each a longitudinal slit, then, by making a pin passing through both rods APp, BC at P to move along the curve BPA, a pencil passing through the intersection of APp, bc will trace out the curve bpA similar to BPA. For, since BP is parallel to bp, therefore

$$AP : Ap :: AB : Ab.$$

1851. (A). The spaces described from rest by a body under the action of any finite force are in the beginning of the motion as the squares of the times in which they are described.

(B). If the force vary as the time from rest, prove that the velocity will vary as the square of the time.

Let the same system be pursued in (B) as is adopted in the Lemma; *i.e.* let AB, BC, CD, &c. represent equal intervals into which the whole time AK is divided.

Let the lines Bb, Cc, Dd, (fig. 68) at right angles to AK represent the magnitudes of the force at the end of the times AB, AC, AD, &c.... Since, by hypothesis, the force varies as the time from rest, the points b, c, d, &c. will all lie in a straight line through A.

If we complete the rectangles Ab, Bc, Cd, &c., these will represent the velocities generated in the intervals AB, BC, CD,... on the supposition that the force remains the same during any interval as it is at the *end* of such interval. Hence, by reasoning similar to that in the Lemma, the limit of the sum of all the rectangles, *i.e.* the triangle AKk, will represent the whole velocity actually generated in the time AK.

Thus we get

$$\text{velocity in time } AK : \text{velocity in time } AD :: \text{area } AKk : \text{area } ADd$$
$$:: AK^2 : Ak^2;$$

i.e. the velocity $\propto$ square of the time.

1850. (A). If a body move in free space under the action of a central force, the velocity at any point of the orbit varies inversely as the perpendicular let fall from the centre upon the tangent.

(B). If lines proportional to the Earth's velocity, and always parallel to the direction of its motion, be drawn from a fixed point, shew that the extremities of these lines will trace out a circle.

Let the lines be drawn from the focus, and let p' be the length of any one of them. Then, since p' is by hypothesis proportional to the Earth's velocity, and by (A), the Earth's velocity is inversely proportional to the perpendicular (p) from the focus on the direction of the Earth's motion, *i.e.* the tangent to the orbit, p' must be proportional to $\frac{1}{p}$, therefore

$$pp' \text{ is constant.}$$

We have then two lines always at right angles to one another, such that their lengths are *symmetrically* related; *i.e.*

so that there is nothing to distinguish one from the other. Now the extremity of p traces out a circle by the property of the ellipse; therefore also the extremity of p' will trace out a circle.

It is clear that the fact stated in (B) having been proved true for lines drawn from the focus, will be true for lines similarly drawn from any fixed point.

1851. (A). If several bodies revolve round a common centre, and the centripetal force vary inversely as the square of the distance, the velocities of the bodies are in a ratio compounded of the ratio of the perpendiculars inversely, and the subduplicate ratio of the latera-recta directly.

(B). The velocity of a body revolving in any conic section is to the velocity of a body revolving in a circle at the distance of half the latus-rectum as that distance is to the perpendicular from the focus upon the tangent.

From (A) we obtain that in any conic section described round a centre of force in the focus varying as $\dfrac{1}{(\text{distance})^2}$,

$$v \propto \frac{L^{\frac{1}{2}}}{p},$$

where p is the perpendicular on the tangent from the focus, and L the semi-latus-rectum.

If u is the velocity of a body moving about the centre of force in a circle whose radius is L, we have $p = L$, and therefore

$$u \propto \frac{L^{\frac{1}{2}}}{L};$$

therefore

$$\frac{v}{u} = \frac{\frac{1}{p}}{\frac{1}{L}} = \frac{L}{p}.$$

1848. (A). The centripetal forces of bodies which describe different circles with uniform velocities tend to the centres of the circles, and are to each other directly as the squares of the arcs described in the same time, and inversely as the radii of the circles.

(B). How much must the length of the day be shortened, in order that the rotation of the Earth may be sufficiently rapid to destroy the weight of bodies at the equator?

Let ω be the angular velocity of the Earth about its axis, or the angle through which it revolves in one second; r the equatoreal radius.

The velocity of any point in the equator $= \omega r$, and therefore, by (A), the centrifugal force on such point due to the Earth's rotation $= \dfrac{(\omega r)^2}{r} = \omega^2 r$. Hence, if f be the force on the same point arising from the attraction of the mass of the Earth,

$$f - \omega^2 r = g.^*$$

Let now ω' be the angular velocity of the Earth when bodies have no weight. Then

$$f - \omega'^2 r = 0,$$

therefore $$(\omega'^2 - \omega^2)\, r = g,$$

$$\omega' = \sqrt{\left(\frac{g}{r} + \omega^2\right)}.$$

Now $\dfrac{\omega}{2\pi} = \dfrac{1}{N}$, if $N =$ number of seconds in a day

$$= 86400;$$

therefore $$\omega = \frac{2\pi}{N};$$

and, if t be the length of the day (in seconds) in the supposed case,

$$\frac{\omega'}{2\pi} = \frac{1}{t},$$

therefore $$\omega' = \frac{2\pi}{t};$$

therefore $$\frac{2\pi}{t} = \sqrt{\left(\frac{g}{r} + \frac{4\pi^2}{N^2}\right)},$$

---

* Observe, it is necessary that ω be the angle described in *one second*, because the expression $g = 32.2$ feet assumes one second to be the unit of time. It must also be noted that r is expressed in *feet*.

therefore $$t = 2\pi N \sqrt{\left(\frac{r}{gN^2 + 4\pi^2 r}\right)},$$

and the number of seconds by which the day must be shortened

$$= N - t$$

$$= N\left\{1 - 2\pi \sqrt{\left(\frac{r}{gN^2 + 4\pi^2 r}\right)}\right\}.$$

1851. (A). The centripetal forces of bodies which describe different circles with uniform velocities, tend to the centres of the circles, and are to each other as the squares of the arcs described in the same time divided by the radii.

(B). Give a formula for finding the height of a body which moves under the attraction of the Earth in such a way as always to be vertically above a point in the equator, stating the numerical values of the quantities appearing in the result.

Let a be the equatoreal radius of the Earth; ω the Earth's angular velocity about its axis; g the force of gravity at the equator; h the height above the Earth's surface of a particle which always remains over a point of the equator.

In order that the body may move in the proposed manner, *i.e.* in order that it may describe a circle of radius $h + a$ with angular velocity ω, the centripetal force must $\propto \frac{(\text{arc})^2}{\text{radius}}$; in fact must $= \frac{(\text{velocity})^2}{\text{radius}} = \frac{\{\omega\,(h+a)\}^2}{h+a} = \omega^2\,(h+a)$.

But the force acting on the body $= g \cdot \frac{a^2}{(h+a)^2}$,

since the attraction of the earth $\propto \frac{1}{(\text{distance})^2}$.

Equating therefore the two expressions for the centripetal force,

$$\omega^2.(h+a) = g \cdot \frac{a^2}{(h+a)^2};$$

or $$(h+a)^3 = \frac{ga^2}{\omega^2},$$

therefore $$h = \left(\frac{ga^2}{\omega^2}\right)^{\frac{1}{3}} - a.$$

In this expression, the numerical value of g in 32·18 feet nearly, of a, 20921665, (because, g being expressed in feet, a must also be expressed in feet), and of ω, $\frac{2\pi}{24 \times 60 \times 60}$ or ·00007272233, (since a *second* is assumed to be the unit of time in the expression for g).

1849. (A). A body describes a parabola under the action of a force parallel to the axis; determine the law of force.

(B). Find the velocity at any point, and the time of moving from the vertex to the extremity of the latus-rectum.

From (A) we obtain that the force $= \frac{2h^2}{CP^2} \cdot \frac{1}{4AS}$, where C (the centre of force) is a point in the axis of the parabola so remote from A, that it may be considered at the same distance from any point of the parabola as from A. Hence the force is constant; let it equal f.

Then, if the velocity at $P = V$,

$$V^2 = \tfrac{1}{2}f.(\text{chord of curvature parallel to the axis}),$$
$$= \tfrac{1}{2}f.4SP,$$
$$= 2f.SP.$$

Again, let t be the time of moving from the vertex to the extremity of the latus-rectum; and V' the velocity at the vertex.

Since the force acts parallel to the axis, it is clear that t will be the time in which a body would describe the semi-latus-rectum with a uniform velocity V',

therefore $$\tfrac{1}{2}L = V't;$$

or $$2AS = t.\sqrt{(2f.AS)},$$

therefore $$t = \sqrt{\left(\frac{2AS}{f}\right)}.$$

1848. (A). Find the law of force tending to the focus of a parabola.

(B). If the latus-rectum of a parabola is 24 feet, and the velocity of a body revolving in it at the vertex is 2 yards per minute, find the time in which the body moves from the vertex to one end of the latus-rectum.

From (A), the force at any point P (fig. 69) of the parabola $= \frac{\mu}{SP^2}$,

where $\mu = \frac{2h^2}{L}$, L being the latus-rectum;

we hence obtain, velocity $= \sqrt{\left(\frac{2\mu}{SP}\right)}$.

Let t be the number of seconds the body takes to move from A to B. Then h being 2 sectorial area described in 1″,

$$t = \frac{2 \text{ area } ASB}{h} = \frac{4}{3}.\frac{AS.SB}{h} = \frac{1}{6}.\frac{L^2}{h},$$

$$= \frac{1}{3\sqrt{2}}.\frac{L^2}{\sqrt{(\mu L)}} = \frac{1}{3\sqrt{2}}.\frac{L^{\frac{3}{2}}}{\sqrt{\mu}}.$$

But $\sqrt{\left(\frac{2\mu}{AS}\right)}$ = velocity at A;

or $\sqrt{\left(\frac{8\mu}{L}\right)} = \frac{1}{10}$, (since 2 yards per minute is $\frac{1}{10}$ of a foot per second),

therefore $t = \frac{20}{3}.\frac{L^{\frac{3}{2}}}{L^{\frac{1}{2}}} = \frac{20}{3}L = \frac{20}{3}.24 = 160$ seconds,

$= 2\frac{2}{3}$ minutes.

1849. (*A*). Find the law of force under the action of which a body may describe an ellipse, one of the foci being the centre of force.

(*B*). If v, v' be the velocities at the extremities of any focal chord, and u that at the extremity of the latus-rectum, then will v^2, u^2, v'^2, be in arithmetical progression.

By (*A*) force to the focus $= \dfrac{\mu}{SP^2}$.

The velocity at any point of the ellipse is that due to $\frac{1}{4}$ of the chord of curvature through the focus;

therefore
$$v^2 = 2 . \frac{\mu}{SP^2} . \frac{PV}{4},$$
$$= \frac{\mu}{SP^2} . \frac{CD^2}{AC},$$
$$= \frac{\mu}{SP^2} . \frac{SP.HP}{AC},$$
$$= \frac{\mu}{SP} . \frac{2AC - SP}{AC},$$
$$= \frac{2\mu}{SP} - \frac{\mu}{AC}.$$

Similarly, if v' be the velocity at the other extremity of the focal chord PSP',
$$v'^2 = \frac{2\mu}{SP'} - \frac{\mu}{AC}.$$

In the same manner, if u is the velocity at the extremity of the latus-rectum and L the semi-length of the latus-rectum,
$$u^2 = \frac{2\mu}{L} - \frac{\mu}{AC}.$$

Hence,
$$v'^2 - u^2 = 2\mu \left(\frac{1}{SP'} - \frac{1}{L}\right),$$
$$u^2 - v^2 = 2\mu \left(\frac{1}{L} - \frac{1}{SP}\right).$$

But by a well-known property of the ellipse,

$$\frac{1}{SP} + \frac{1}{SP'} = \frac{2}{L};$$

therefore $$\frac{1}{SP'} - \frac{1}{L} = \frac{1}{L} - \frac{1}{SP};$$

therefore $$v'^2 - u^2 = u^2 - v^2,$$

or v^2, u^2, v'^2, are in arithmetical progression.

EXAMPLES FOR PRACTICE.

EUCLID.

(A). Book I. prop. 26.

(B). The sides AB, AC of a right-angled triangle, in which A is the right angle, are produced; if the lines bisecting the exterior angles meet in O, and perpendiculars be drawn to the sides produced, shew that the figure $OMAN$ is a square.

(A). Book I. prop. 32.

(B). A semicircle $ABDC$ is trisected by the straight lines OB, OD drawn from the centre O; shew that the line joining B, C bisects OD.

(A). Book I. prop. 34.

(B). Shew that any straight line passing through the middle point of the diameter of a parallelogram bisects the parallelogram.

(A). Book I. prop. 39.

(B). Two straight lines AC, BD, cut in E. If the triangle ABE equal the triangle CED, and the triangle AED equal the triangle BEC, the figure $ABCD$ is a parallelogram.

(A). Book III. prop. 11.

(B). If two circles touch each other internally, and any circle be described touching both, prove that the sum of the distances of its centre from the centres of the two given circles will be invariable.

(A). Book III. prop. 22.

(B). If all the angles of a quadrilateral inscribed in a circle are bisected by the diagonals, it must be a square.

(C). If circles be described about the four triangles formed by the intersection of four straight lines, shew that these circles all pass through one point.

(A). Book III. prop. 26.

(B). If a circle be described about a triangle ABC, and perpendiculars be let fall from the points A, B, C on the opposite sides of the triangle, and be produced to meet the circle in D, E, F, respectively; shew that the arcs EF, FD, DE are bisected in A, B, C.

(A). Book III. prop. 31.

(B). Two equal circles cut one another in A and B; if the diameters AC, AD be drawn in the two circles, shew that CB, BD are in the same straight line. Also, if the diameter DA of one centre be produced to meet the other in E, shew that E is a point in the circle described with centre B and radius BD.

(A). Book III. prop. 32.

(B). A point A is taken in a circle such that, if the tangents AB, AC be drawn to an equal circle, and be produced backwards to meet the former circle in D and E, the chord $DE = BC$. Shew that the triangle ABC is equilateral.

(A). Book III. prop. 36.

(B). $ABCD$ is a quadrilateral inscribed in a circle, such that the sides AB, DC produced, and the sides AD, BC produced, meet respectively in two points E, F of a concentric circle. Shew that EF cannot be parallel to BD unless each of the angles ABC, ADC are right angles.

(C). If two circles cut one another, then the common chord produced bisects their common tangent.

(A). Book IV. prop. 15.

(B). Six equal circles pass through one point, so as by their mutual intersections to determine the angular points of two regular hexagons. Shew that of the two circles circumscribing these hexagons, one is equal to any one of the given circles, and the area of the other is three times the area of any one of them.

GEOMETRICAL CONIC SECTIONS.

(A). The tangent at any point of a parabola makes equal angles with the axis and with the line joining the point with the focus.

(B). If the diameter at the point P in a parabola be produced to meet the directrix in M, and MS be drawn to the focus S, then the perpendicular from P on MS will be a tangent at P.

(C). Draw a pair of tangents to a parabola from a given point in the directrix.

(A). If from the focus (S) of a parabola whose vertex is A, SY be drawn perpendicular to the tangent PT, prove that AY is the tangent at the vertex.

(B). In SP a point A' is taken so that $SA' = SA$; shew that $SA'.A'P = AY^2$.

(A). Define an ellipse.

(B). Supposing no bodies to exist in space but the sun and a small plane mirror which moves so as always to be a tangent to its path, find the locus of the sun's image.

(A). The rectangle under the abscissæ of the axis-major of an ellipse is to the square of the semi-ordinate as the square of the axis-major to the square of the axis-minor ($AN.NM : PN^2 :: AC^2 : BC^2$).

(B). Produce NP to meet the auxiliary circle in Q; draw PR parallel to QC, meeting the axis-major in R. Shew that $PR = BC$.

(*A*). In the ellipse $CP^2 + CD^2 = AC^2 + BC^2$.

(*B*). If on AB as diameter a circle be described, and AQ drawn to the circumference be equal to any semi-diameter of the ellipse, shew that BQ will be equal to the semi-diameter conjugate to it.

(*A*). Define an hyperbola.

(*B*). In a triangle with given base a circle is inscribed touching the base in a fixed point; prove that the locus of the vertex is an hyperbola.

(*A*). The locus of a point whose distances from two given points is constant is a circle.

(*B*). Given the directrix and two points of a conic section, shew that the locus of the focus is a circle.

ALGEBRA.

(*A*). Divide $1 - x^n$ by $1 - x$.

(*B*). Expand $(1+x).(1+x^2)(1+x^4)(1+x^8)\ldots\ldots(1+x^{2^r})$ in ascending powers of x.

(*A*). If a, b, represent the sides of a rectangle, explain in what sense the area is represented by ab.

(*B*). The length of a rectangular field exceeds the breadth by one yard, and the area is three acres; find the length of the sides.

(*A*). $x^2 + y^2$ is always $> 2xy$.

(*B*). Shew that

$$\sqrt{\left(\frac{a^3}{bc}\right)} + \sqrt{\left(\frac{b^3}{ac}\right)} + \sqrt{\left(\frac{c^3}{ab}\right)}$$

is never $< \sqrt{a} + \sqrt{b} + \sqrt{c}$.

(*A*). If $\frac{a}{b} = \frac{c}{d}$, prove that $\frac{a \pm c}{b \pm a}$ is equal to either.

(*B*). Eliminate a from the equations

$$\frac{x}{a^2 + x^2} = \frac{2y}{a^2 + y^2} = \frac{4z}{a^2 + z^2}.$$

(*A*). Find the sum of an arithmetic series.

(*B*). m arithmetic series have the same common difference 1, their first terms are $1, r, r^2, \ldots r^{m-1}$, and the numbers of their terms are $r - 1, r(r-1), r^2(r-1), \ldots r^{m-1}(r-1)$. Find the sum of all the series.

(*A*). Find the sum of an infinite geometric series, whose common ratio is < 1.

(*B*). The sides of a square are divided in order in the ratio of $m : 1 - m$; the square formed by joining the points of division is treated in the same manner, and so on. Shew that the sum of the areas of all the squares to infinity is $\frac{a^2}{2m(1-m)}$; a being a side of the original square.

(*A*). Investigate the number of combinations of n things r together.

(*B*). If ${}_nC_r$ represent the number, shew that

$${}_nC_r + n_nC_{r-1} + n \cdot \frac{n-1}{2} \cdot {}_nC_{r-2} + \ldots = {}_{2n}C_r.$$

(*A*). Write down the general term of $(1 + x)^m$.

(*B*). If ${}_mA_r$ represent the coefficient of x^r, shew that

$${}_mA_2 + {}_mA_1 \cdot {}_mA_3 + {}_mA_2 \cdot {}_mA_3 + \ldots = {}_{2m}A_{m+2}.$$

(*A*). Prove that the discount on a sum of money is half the harmonic mean between the principal and interest.

(*B*). The interest on a certain sum of money is £180, and the discount on the same sum for the same time and at the same rate of interest is £150; find the sum.

TRIGONOMETRY.

(*A*). Trisect an angle whose cosine is given.

(*B*). If β be any angle,

$$\cos\frac{2\pi-\beta}{3}+\cos\frac{\beta}{3}+\cos\frac{2\pi+\beta}{3}=0.$$

(*A*). Express the tangent of an angle of a triangle in terms of the sides.

(*B*). Prove the formula,

$$1-\tan\frac{A}{2}.\tan\frac{B}{2}=\frac{2c}{a+b+c}.$$

(*A*). Express the cosine of half an angle of a triangle in terms of the sides.

(*B*). If A', B', C' be the angles which the sides of a triangle subtend at the centre of the inscribed circle, then will

$$\sin A'.\sin B'.\sin C'=\sin A+\sin B+\sin C.$$

(*A*). Find the area of a triangle, (1) in terms of a side and the perpendicular upon the opposite angle, (2) in terms of two sides and the included angle.

(*B*). If (a) be the side of a regular polygon of n sides, and if perpendiculars (p) be drawn from any point in the polygon to the sides, shew that

$$a=\frac{2}{n}.\Sigma(p).\tan\frac{\pi}{n}.$$

(*A*). Express the area of a triangle in terms of the sides.

(*B*). Required the sides of a triangle whose area is 24 square feet, and sides in the ratio 3 : 4 : 5.

(*A*). Find the sum of the sines of a series of angles in arithmetical progression.

(*B*). If $2n$ lines of length (a) be drawn from a point, so that every adjacent two include the same angle, shew that the sum of all the triangles of different magnitude which can be formed by joining the extremities of the lines is $\frac{a^2}{2}.\cot\frac{\pi}{2n}$.

(*A*). If θ be the circular measure of an angle, the limiting value to which $\frac{\sin\theta}{\theta}$ approaches when θ approaches 0, is 1.

(*B*). If the unit of angular measurement be an angle of $60°$, shew that the limit of $\frac{\sin\theta}{\theta}$ when $\theta = 0$, will be 1·04719....

STATICS.

(*A*). Distinguish between a particle and a rigid body. What kind of motion is each capable of?

(*B*). A particle is attached to a fixed point, (1) by means of a string, (2) by means of a rigid rod; what will be the conditions of equilibrium in the two cases, when given forces act in the direction of the string or rod, and perpendicular to it?

(*A*). Equilibrium takes place on a straight lever when the arms are inversely as the forces.

(*B*). Compare the weights of a sphere of given radius, when weighed by suspending it from one end of a balance, (1) by a string, (2) by a rod without weight which is glued to the sphere.

(*A*). Prove the parallelogram of forces.

(*B*). Every point of the rim of a hemispherical bowl repels with a force varying as the distance; shew that a particle will rest at any point of the inner surface of the bowl.

(*A*). Explain the nature of the reaction of smooth surfaces.

(*B*). A tube in the form of a parabola is placed with its axis vertical, the curve lying above the tangent at its vertex. A heavy particle is placed in the tube, and a repulsive force acts along the ordinate upon the particle: find the law of force in order that it may sustain the particle in any position.

(*A*). Any number of forces act in the same plane on a point: find the conditions of equilibrium.

(*B*). A particle is placed on a smooth square table (whose side is a) at distances c_1, c_2, c_3, c_4, from the corners, and to it are attached strings passing over smooth pulleys at the corners and supporting weights P_1, P_2, P_3, P_4; shew that if there is equilibrium,

$$\left(\frac{P_1}{c_1}+\frac{P_2}{c_2}+\frac{P_3}{c_3}+\frac{P_4}{c_4}\right)\cdot\frac{c_1^{\,2}-c_3^{\,2}}{a^2}=2\left(\frac{P_3}{c_3}-\frac{P_1}{c_1}\right).$$

(*A*). If three forces keep a rigid body at rest, their directions are either parallel or meet in a point.

(*B*). A square lamina is suspended by two strings of given length fastened to a fixed point, and to two given points in the sides of the square: find the position in which it will hang.

(*C*). A wheel, whose centre of gravity is not in its centre, is kept at rest on a perfectly rough inclined plane by a given horizontal force applied at the centre: find the amount of friction.

(*A*). Find the centre of gravity of a plane triangle.

(*B*). If the sides of the triangle be bisected, and the triangle, formed by joining these points, be removed; shew that the centre of gravity of the remainder will coincide with that of the whole triangle.

(*C*). How does it appear from mechanical considerations that the lines joining the angular points of a triangle with the bisections of the opposite sides intersect in the same point?

(*A*). Find $\frac{W}{P}$ in the wheel and axle.

(*B*). What weight suspended from the axle can be supported by $1\frac{1}{2}$ lbs. suspended from the wheel, if the radius of the axle is $1\frac{1}{2}$ feet and the radius of the wheel is $3\frac{1}{4}$ feet?

(*A*). Find $\frac{W}{P}$ in the system of pullies where the same string passes round all the pullies.

(*B*). Two weights W_1, W_2, are attached to two such systems, having n_1, n_2 parallel strings respectively; find the ratio $W_1 : W_2$, (1) when the weights are hung from the lower blocks, the same string passing round both systems; (2) when hung from the upper block, the lower blocks being connected by a string passing under a smooth fixed pulley.

(*A*). Find the resultant of two couples acting in different planes.

(*B*). Three couples of equal moment (m) tend to make a rigid body revolve about three lines drawn from a point, the middle one making equal angles (α) with the other two; shew that the moment of the resultant couple is

$$m(1 + 2\cos\alpha).$$

DYNAMICS.

(*A*). How is velocity measured?

(*B*). If 1″ is the unit of time, and 1 foot unit of length, what will be the numerical expression for the velocity of a carriage, one of whose wheels, of 18 inches radius, makes two revolutions in a minute?

(*A*). What is the connexion between angular and linear velocity?

(*B*). A train moves from one station to another along a curve, and appears to an observer equidistant from each station to move uniformly from one to the other in a given time: find the velocity of the train when nearest to the observer.

(*A*). Explain what is meant by resolved velocities.

(*B*). A man in a train moving at the rate of m miles an hour throws a stone at the rate of n miles an hour perpendicularly to the direction of the train, so as to hit a post c yards distant from the railway. Shew that his distance from the post at the instant of throwing the stone is

$$\frac{c(m^2+n^2)^{\frac{1}{2}}}{n} \text{ yards.}$$

(*A*). The velocity acquired by a body in falling down a curve is that due to the same vertical height.

(*B*). A body begins to move from the highest point of a vertical circular tube. Find the velocity when it has fallen through a length (s) of the tube.

(*C*). AB is the vertical diameter of a sphere; a chord is drawn from A meeting the surface in P, and the tangent plane at B in Q; shew that the time down PQ varies as BQ, and the velocity acquired varies as BP.

(*A*). The velocity at any point of the parabolic path of a projectile is that due to the distance of that point from the directrix.

(*B*). If V be the velocity at any point P, and v the velocity attained by a body falling down SP as an inclined plane; shew that $V^2 - v^2$ is constant and $= g$ (latus-rectum).

(*C*). The least velocity which is sufficient to project a body over a cube standing on the horizontal plane through the point of projection and whose edge is $2a$, is that due to the height $3a$, the angle of projection is $\cos^{-1}\frac{1}{\sqrt{6}}$, and the point of projection is at a distance $a(\sqrt{5}-1)$ from one of the sides of the cube.

HYDROSTATICS.

(*A*). Given the specific gravities of two fluids, given volumes of which are mixed: find the specific gravity of the compound.

(*B*). What weight of water must be added to a pound of a fluid whose specific gravity is $\frac{1}{2}$, in order that the specific gravity of the mixture may be $\frac{3}{4}$?

(*A*). Shew that the pressure on any horizontal area below the surface of a fluid depends only on its depth below the surface, and not at all on the form of the vessel in which it is contained.

(*B*). The same quantity of fluid which will just fill a hollow cone, is poured into a cylinder whose base is equal to that of the cone: compare the pressures on the bases.

(*A*). The surface of a heavy fluid at rest is a horizontal plane.

(*B*). If beside gravity a constant accelerating force (f) acted in a horizontal direction on every particle of the fluid, what would be the form of the surface?

(*A*). How is it shewn that the pressure of air under a constant temperature varies as the density?

(*B*). A piston fits closely in a cylinder, of which a length a below the piston contains atmospheric air: compare the forces sufficient to draw out the piston through a distance b, with that sufficient to push it in through the same distance.

(*A*). Investigate the conditions that a body may float.

(*B*). A heavy body floats between two fluids; V_1, V_2 are the volumes immersed, F_1, F_2 the forces which would keep it at rest when entirely immersed in the first and second fluid respectively: prove that $F_1V_1 = F_2V_2$.

OPTICS.

(*A*). State the law of reflexion.

(*B*). Given the position of two small mirrors, find the position of an eye which sees itself by reflection in both mirrors.

(*A*). Explain what is meant by the critical angle.

(*B*). An open cylinder is polished internally and filled with water: shew that any ray which enters the water will after a number of reflections emerge again at the surface of the water.

(*A*.) Determine the geometrical focus of a pencil of rays which falls on a plane refracting surface.

(*B*). Find the depth of a pond which appears to be 6 feet deep to a person looking directly down upon it. ($\mu = \frac{4}{3}$ for water.)

(*A*). Find the geometrical focus of a pencil of rays after direct refraction at a spherical refracting surface.

(*B*). Rays are incident parallel to the axis on a glass cylinder with hemispherical ends: find the geometrical focus.

(*A*). Prove that if f be the focal length of a lens,

$$\frac{1}{f} = (\mu - 1) . \left(\frac{1}{r} - \frac{1}{s}\right) .$$

(*B*). If the refractive indices from air to glass and water be respectively $\frac{3}{2}$ and $\frac{4}{3}$, in what proportion is the focal length of a glass lens altered by being used under water?

(*A*). Describe Ramsden's Eye-piece.

(*B*). Construct one with glass ($\mu = \frac{3}{2}$) by which a magnifying power of 200 may be obtained with an astronomical telescope whose object-glass is of 6 feet focal-length.

NEWTON.

(*A*). Prove Newton's Fourth Lemma.

(*B*). Compare the areas of two ellipses which have their minor axes equal.

(*A*.) In central orbits the velocity varies inversely as the perpendicular from the centre of force upon the tangent. (Sect. ii., Prop. 1., Cor.)

(B). If a body describe an ellipse round a centre of force in the focus, shew that the sum of the reciprocals of the squares of the velocities at the extremities of any chord passing through the other focus is constant.*

(A). A body moves in a parabola, find the law of force tending to the focus.

(B). If at any point the direction of its motion were changed without altering its velocity, what curve would it describe?

(A). If a body describe the arc PQ of its orbit in T'', and QR be a subtense parallel to the direction of the force at P, the force $= 2$ limit $\frac{QR}{T^2}$.

(B). Find the force towards the centre required to make a body move in a circle whose radius is 5 feet, with such a velocity as to complete a revolution in 5 seconds.

(A). A body under the action of a central force varying directly as the distance will describe an ellipse, with the centre of force as centre. (Sect. ii., Prop. x., Cor.)

(B). A body (P) is suspended from a fixed point (A) by an elastic string which passes through a smooth ring (B) vertically under A, so that the distance AB equals the natural length of the string. Assuming that the extension of an elastic string is proportional to the force which stretches it, determine, if P be set in motion, what curve it will describe.

---

* See Ferrers and Jackson's *Solutions of Senate-House Problems*, p. 51.

THE END.

CAMBRIDGE;
PRINTED BY METCALFE AND PALMER.

PLATE I.

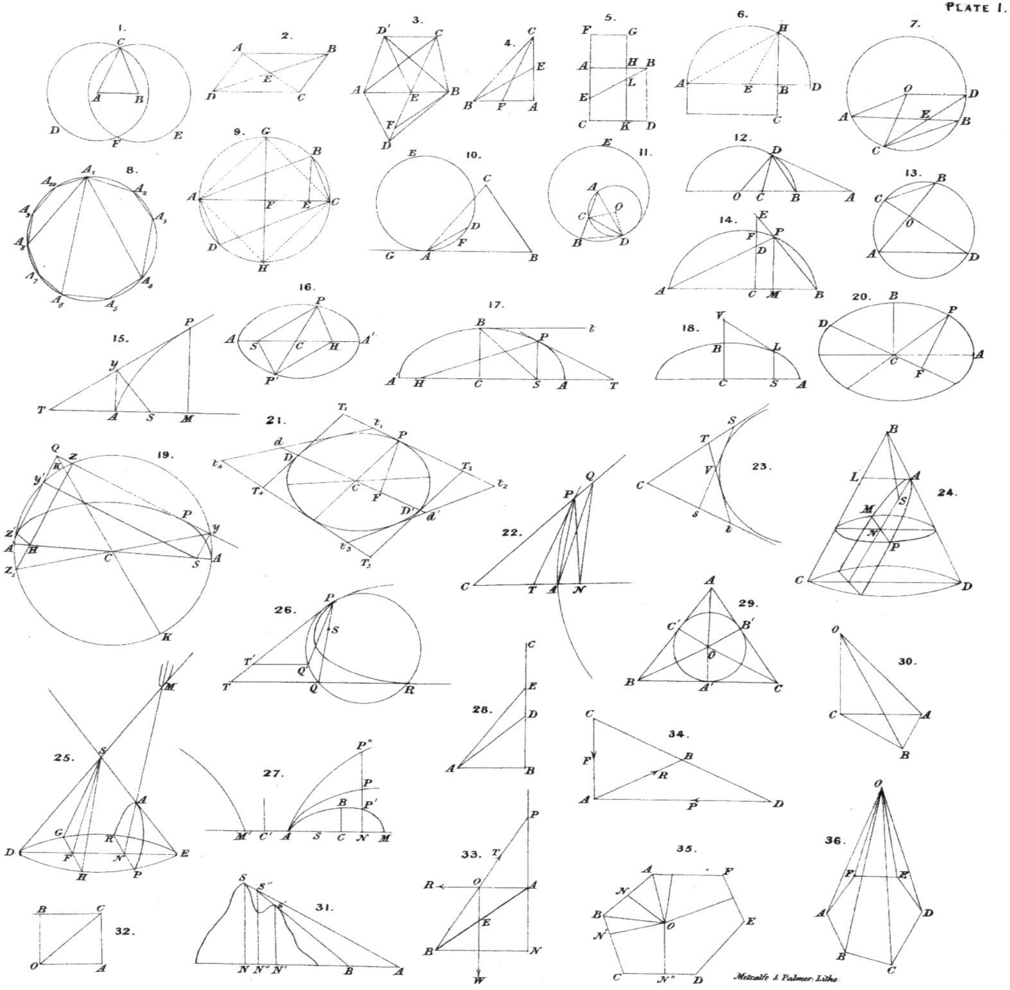

Metcalfe & Palmer, Litho.

Plate 2.

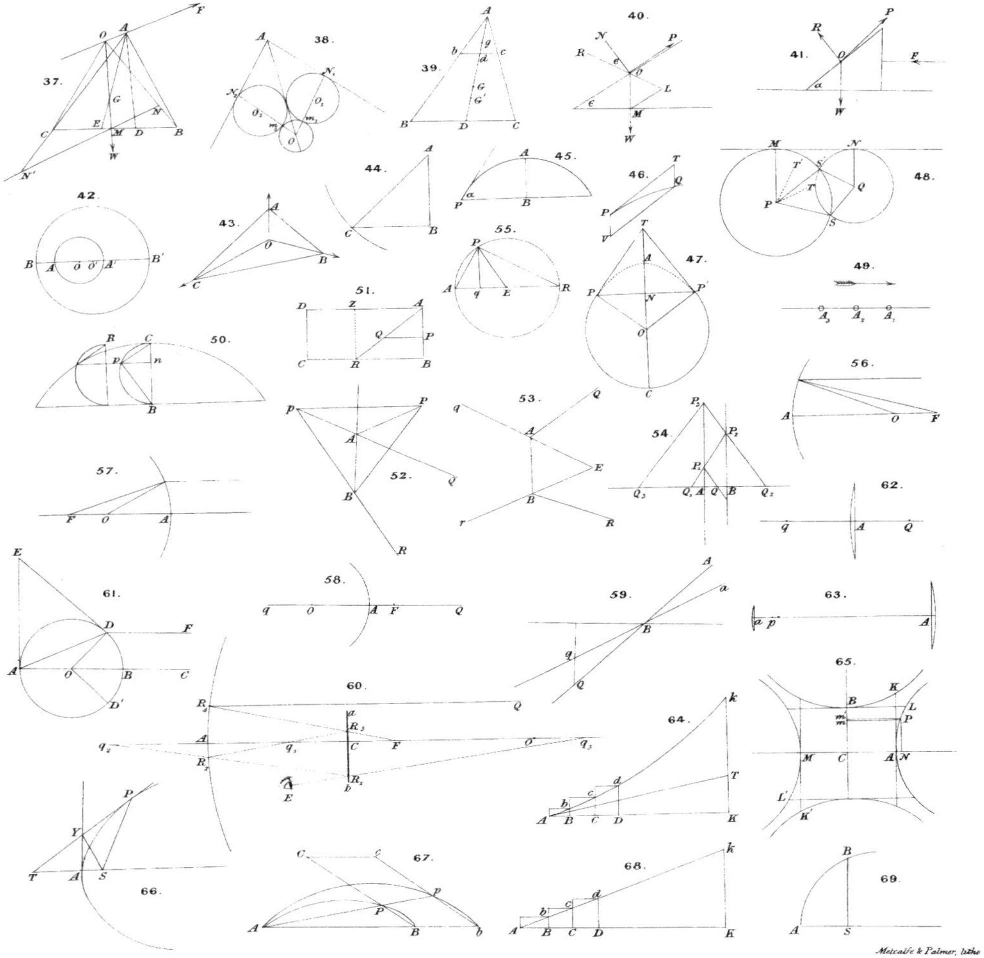

Metcalfe & Palmer, litho

Cambridge.

Cambridge Customs and Costumes.

Containing upwards of one hundred and fifty (humorous) Vignettes. 3s. 6d.

Cambridge Guide:

Including Historical and Architectural Notices of the Public Buildings, and a concise account of the Customs and Ceremonies of the University. With a sketch of the Places most worthy of remark in the County. A New Edition, with Engravings and a Map. Royal 18mo. cloth, 5s. 6d.

Edited by W. *THOMSON*, M.A.,

Fellow of St. Peter's College, Cambridge, and Professor of Natural Philosophy in the University of Glasgow.

Cambridge and Dublin Mathematical Journal,

Vols. I., II., III., IV., V., and VI. 8vo. cloth, price 16s. each.

Also recently published, a second Edition of the Cambridge Mathematical Journal, Vol. I.; being the First Series of the above Work. 8vo. cloth, 18s.

" This Periodical will be found to contain contributions by most of the first Mathematicians of both Universities to all branches of the Science, including many that will be found useful to the Student in the course of his Academical career, and interesting to the more advanced Investigator.

Edited by the Rev. A. P. *MOOR*, M.A.,

of Trinity College, Cambridge, and Sub-Warden of St. Augustine's College, Canterbury.

Cambridge Theological Papers.

Comprising those given at the Voluntary Theological and the Crosse Scholarship Examinations. Edited with References and Indices. 8vo. bds. 7s. 6d.

This will be found a very useful help to reading for the Voluntary Theological and for Ordination Examinations.

By the Rev. J. J. *SMITH*, M.A.,

late Senior Fellow of Gonville and Caius College, Cambridge.

Caius College, Cambridge.

A Catalogue of the MSS. in the Library of Gonville and Caius College, Cambridge. 8vo. cloth, 10s. 6d.

CICERO.

1.

On Old Age.

Literally Translated, with Notes. By a Master of Arts. 12mo. sewed, 2s. 6d.

2.

On Friendship.

Literally Translated, with Notes. By a Master of Arts. 12mo. sewed, 2s. 6d.

By the Rev. C. *CLAYTON*, M.A.,
Senior Fellow and Tutor of Gonville & Caius College, Cambridge.

Parochial Sermons,

Preached at Chatham and Rochester. Second Edition, 12mo. cloth, 6s.

By G. *CURREY*, B.D.,
Preacher at the Charterhouse and Boyle Lecturer, formerly Fellow of St. John's College, Cambridge.

Hulsean Lectures for 1851:

The Preparation for the Gospel as exhibited in the History of the Israelites.

By the Rev. J. W. *COLENSO*, M.A.,
late Fellow of St. John's College, Cambridge.

Cottage Family Prayers.

12mo. sewed, 3d.

By PATRICK *COLQUHOUN*, Juris utriusque Doctor, M.A.,
St. John's College, Cambridge;
Barrister-at-Law, Inner Temple; &c. &c.

A Summary of the Roman Civil Law;

Illustrated by Commentaries on and Parallels from the Mosaic, Canon, Mohammedan, English, and Foreign Law. Part I. 8vo. sewed, 10s. 6d. Part II., 12s. 6d. The two Parts in one Vol., bds. £1 4s.

By J. E. *COOPER*, M.A.,
Fellow of St. John's College, Cambridge.

A Geometrical Treatise on the Conic Sections;

With an Appendix, containing the first Nine and the Eleventh of Newton's Lemmas: intended chiefly as an Introduction to the Geometrical Doctrine of Limits. *Preparing.*

The Clergy and the Commons:
Or the Right of the National Convocation to sit in Parliament Vindicated. 8vo. 1s.

DEMOSTHENES.

1.

De Corona.
The Greek Text, with English Explanatory Notes. By B. W. F. DRAKE, M.A., Fellow of King's College, Cambridge. Crown 8vo. cloth, 5s.

"*The Editor has diligently availed himself of the best modern sources, and has in a brief space given such information as will enable a student to read the original with comparative ease. The Grammatical difficulties in the text are well explained, and frequent references are given, for the elucidation of the historical and archæological subjects alluded to by the Orator.*"
LITERARY GAZETTE.

"*Useful notes.*"—THE GUARDIAN.

"*A neat and useful Edition.*"—ATHENÆUM.

2.

The Oration on the Crown,
Literally Translated into English by the Rev. J. P. NORRIS, M.A., Fellow of Trinity College, Cambridge, and one of Her Majesty's Inspectors of Schools. Crown 8vo. sewed, 3s.

"*The best translation that we remember to have seen.*"
LITERARY GAZETTE.

"*Very accurate.*"—THE GUARDIAN.

Edited by the Rev. Dr. *DONALDSON*,
Head-Master of King Edward's School, Bury St. Edmund's, and formerly Fellow of Trinity College, Cambridge.

The Theatre of the Greeks.
A series of Papers relating to the History and Criticism of the Greek Drama. With an original Introduction and Notes. Sixth Edition revised. 8vo. cloth, 15s.

EUCLID.

Enunciations and Corollaries of the Propositions of the first Six Books of Euclid, together with the Eleventh and Twelfth. 24mo. sewed, 1s.

By N. M. *FERRERS*, B.A., and J. S. *JACKSON*, B.A.,
of Caius College, Cambridge.

Solutions of the Senate-House Problems from 1848 to 1851.
8vo. cloth, 15s. 6d.

By THOMAS *FULLER.*

The History of the University of Cambridge, since the
Conquest. A new Edition, with additional Notes, and a beautiful Map. By the late Rev. M. PRICKETT, M.A., F.S.A., late Chaplain of Trinity College; and THOMAS WRIGHT, Esq., M.A., F.S.A., of the same College. 8vo. cloth bds. 12s.

"*Next to Shakspeare.*"—S. T. COLERIDGE.

"*His way of telling a story, for its eager liveliness, and perpetual running commentary of the narrator happily blended with the narration, is perhaps unrivalled.*"—CHARLES LAMB.

"*In him learning was but subsidiary to wit, and wit but secondary to wisdom.*"—RETROSPECTIVE REVIEW.

By the Rev. A. R. *GRANT,* M.A.,
Fellow of Trinity College, Cambridge.

Plane Astronomy.
Including Explanations of Celestial Phenomena and Descriptions of Astronomical Instruments. 8vo. bds. 6s.

By the Rev. W. N. *GRIFFIN,* M.A.,
late Fellow and Assistant Tutor of St. John's College, Cambridge.

1.

The Theory of Double Refraction.
8vo. sewed, 2s.

2.

A Treatise on Optics.
8vo. bds. 8s.

By the Rev. J. *HARRIS,* M.A.,
of Catharine Hall, Cambridge.

Questions in Arithmetic.
With an Appendix, containing Problems in Mechanics and Hydrostatics. Crown 8vo. 3s. 6d.

BP. *HALLIFAX.*

An Analysis of the Civil Law,
In which a Comparison is occasionally made between the Roman Laws and those of England. A new Edition, with alterations and additions, being the Heads of a Course of Lectures publicly read in the University of Cambridge. By J. W. GELDART, LL.D. 8vo. cloth bds. 8s. 6d. Interleaved, 10s. 6d. Double interleaved, 12s. 6d.

By G. W. *HEMMING,* M.A.,
Fellow of St. John's College, Cambridge.

An Elementary Treatise on the Differential and Integral
Calculus. 8vo. bds. 9s.

MACMILLAN & CO.'S PUBLICATIONS,

ARISTOPHANES.

A Commentary on the Works of Aristophanes.
By W. G. CLARK, M.A., Fellow and Assistant Tutor of Trinity College, Cambridge. *In Preparation.*

ARISTOTLE.

The Rhetoric of Aristotle;
The Greek Text: with English Notes, Critical and Explanatory. *Preparing.*

ÆSCHYLUS.

A Translation into English Verse of the Prometheus Vinctus of Æschylus. With an Introduction and Notes. By C. G. PROWETT, M.A., Fellow of Caius College. 8vo. sewed, 3s. 6d.

By the Rev. CHURCHILL *BABINGTON*, M.A.,
Fellow of St. John's College, Cambridge.

Mr. Macaulay's Character of the Clergy in the latter part of the Seventeenth Century, considered. 8vo. bds. 4s. 6d.

> "*Apart from its triumphant conclusion, a very finished piece of Criticism.*"—CHRISTIAN REMEMBRANCER.

THE *BAKER* MSS.

Index to the Manuscripts of Thomas Baker, (formerly Fellow of St. John's College, Cambridge,) which are preserved in the British Museum and in the Library of the University of Cambridge. 8vo. bds. 7s. 6d.

> "*These Manuscripts consist of transcripts of original documents various in kind, such as Charters, Statutes of Corporate Bodies, Wills, Royal and other Letters, Monastic, College, and University Registers, Historical and Biographical Notices of Authors and their works, &c.; the whole selected with remarkable judgment, so as to form an invaluable store of information otherwise unattainable.*"—PREFACE.

By the Rev. E. H. *BICKERSTETH,* M.A.,
of Trinity College, Cambridge.

Poems: including those which obtained the Chancellor's Medal for the Years 1844-45-46. In foolscap 8vo., cloth, 6s.

By JOHN H. *BOARDMAN,* M.A.,
Fellow of Gonville and Caius College, Cambridge, and Mathematical Master in the Grammar School, Manchester.

1.

Arithmetic: Rules and Reasons. 12mo. cloth, 2s. 6d.

2.

Arithmetical Examples. 12mo. cloth, 1s. 6d.

3.

Arithmetic; and Arithmetical Examples: being the above works bound together. 12mo. cloth, 3s. 6d.

4.

Arithmetical Examples; and Key. 12mo. cloth, 2s. 6d.

5.

Arithmetic: Rules and Reasons; Arithmetical Examples: and the Key. Bound in one volume, 12mo., cloth, 4s.

By Professor *BOOLE.*

The Mathematical Analysis of Logic.
Being an Essay towards a Calculus of Deductive Reasoning. 8vo. sewed, 5s.

Burney Prize Essay.

1.

FORBES, Rev. G. H., for 1847. 8vo. bds. 5s. 6d.
Subject—"The Goodness of God."

2.

PRESCOTT, G. F. (B.A., Scholar of Trinity College, Cambridge,) for 1850.
Subject—"The Unity of Design, which pervades the successive dispensations of Religion recorded in the Scriptures; an argument for the Truth of Revelation." *Shortly.*

Bp. *BUTLER.*

Butler's Analogy, an Analysis of.
By the Rev. J. P. Parkinson, D.C.L., late Fellow of Magdalen College, Oxford. Second Edition. 12mo. cloth, 2s.

Cambridge.

By the Rev. J. S. *HENSLOW*, M.A., Professor of Botany.

1.

Syllabus of a Course of Lectures on Botany,
Suggesting matter for a Pass-Examination at Cambridge in this Subject. 8vo. sewed, 1s. 6d.

2.

Questions on the Subject-Matter of Sixteen Lectures in Botany, required for a Pass-Examination. 8vo. sewed, 1s.

HIERURGIA ANGLICANA.

Documents and Extracts illustrative of the Ritual of the Church of England after the Reformation. With Illustrations. Edited by Members of the Cambridge Camden Society. 8vo. cloth, 13s.

By the Rev. JOHN *HIND*, M.A., F.C.P.S., F.R.A.S.,
late Fellow and Tutor of Sidney Sussex College, Cambridge.

1.

An Introduction to the Elements of Algebra.
Being a Sequel to the Principles and Practice of Arithmetic. Designed for the use of Students. Third Edition. 12mo. cloth bds. 5s.

2.

The Elements of Algebra.
Designed for the use of Students in the University. Fifth Edition. 8vo. cloth bds. 12s. 6d.

3.

The Principles and Practice of Arithmetic.
12mo. cloth bds. 4s. 6d.

"*Mr. Hind's Arithmetic in the later editions appears to me to be drawn up in such a manner as to be suited for use in Schools for those who are intended to go to the University. It includes the use of Logarithms, and the mensuration of various figures, (triangles, circles, &c.) which I have spoken of as desirable appendages to the parts of Arithmetic usually learnt in Schools.*"
DR. WHEWELL, *Cambridge Studies*, p. 228.

4.

The Solutions of the Questions attended with any difficulty in the Principles and Practice of Arithmetic. With an Appendix containing Questions for Examination in all the Rules of Arithmetic. Second Edition. *Preparing.*

5.

The Elements of Plane and Spherical Trigonometry;
With the Nature and Properties of Logarithms, and the Construction and the Use of Mathematical Tables. Designed for the use of Students in the University. A New Edition. *Preparing.*

Hulsean Prize Essay.

1.

GRUGGEN, F. J., for 1844. 8vo. sewed, 3s. 6d.

Subject—"The Lawfulness and Obligation of Oaths."

2.

BABINGTON, CHURCHILL, for 1845. 8vo. bds. 5s.

Subject—"The Influences of Christianity in promoting the Abolition of Slavery in Europe."

3.

WROTH, H. T., for 1848. 8vo. sewed, 3s.

Subject—"Mahommedanism considered in relation to Christian Evidence."

4.

MACKENZIE, H., for 1850.

Subject—"The beneficial influence of the Christian Clergy during the first thousand years of the Christian Era." *Preparing.*

By the Rev. J. *HYMERS*, D.D.,
Fellow and Tutor of St. John's College, Cambridge.

1.

A Treatise on Analytical Geometry of Three Dimensions.
Containing the Theory of Curve Surfaces. Third Edition. 8vo. bds. 10s. 6d.

2.

Elements of the Theory of Astronomy.
Second Edition. 8vo. bds. 14s.

3.

A Treatise on Conic Sections, and the Application of Algebra to Geometry. Third Edition. 8vo. bds. 9s.

4.

A Treatise on the Theory of Algebraical Equations.
Second Edition. 8vo. bds. 9s. 6d.

5.

A Treatise on Differential Equations and on the Calculus of Finite Differences. 8vo. bds. 10s.

6.

A Treatise on Plane and Spherical Trigonometry, and on Trigonometrical Tables and Logarithms; together with a selection of Problems, and their Solutions. Third Edition, altered and enlarged. 8vo. bds. 8s. 6d.

7.

A Treatise on the Integral Calculus.
Containing the Integration of Explicit Functions of one Variable; together with the Theory of Definite Integrals and of Elliptic Functions. Third Edition, revised and enlarged. 8vo. bds. 10s. 6d.

HUME and SMOLLETT.

History of England.
10 vols. 8vo. cloth, (best Trade Edition,) £4.

HYPERIDES,

The Oration of, against Demosthenes, respecting the Treasure of Harpalus. The fragments of the Greek Text, now first edited from the Facsimile of the MS. discovered at Egyptian Thebes in 1847; together with other fragments of the same Oration, cited in ancient Greek writers. With a previous dissertation and Notes, and Facsimile of a portion of the MS. By CHURCHILL BABINGTON, M.A., Fellow of St. John's College. 4to. sewed, 6s. 6d.

By F. J. *JAMESON,* B.A.,
of Caius College, Cambridge.

The Principles of the Solutions of the Senate-House 'Riders'
Exemplified in the Solution of those proposed in the years 1848 to 1851. *Just Ready.*

By the Rev. LEONARD *JENYNS,* M.A.

A Manual of British Vertebrate Animals,
Or Descriptions of all the Animals belonging to the classes, Mammalia, Aves, Reptilia, Amphibia, and Pisces, which have hitherto been observed in the British Islands. Including the Domesticated, Naturalized, and Extirpated Species: the whole systematically arranged. 8vo. bds. 13s.

BP. *JEWELL.*

1.

Apologia Ecclesiæ Anglicanæ.
Huic Novæ Editioni accedit Epistola celeberrima ad Virum Nobilem D. Scipionem, Patricium Venetum, de Concilio Tridentino conscripta. Fcap. 8vo. bds. 4s. 6d.

2.

An Apology of the Church of England,
And an Epistle to Seignior Scipio concerning the Council of Trent, translated from the original Latin, and illustrated with Notes drawn chiefly from the Author's "Defence of the Apology." By the Rev. A. T. RUSSELL, B.C.L. Fcap. 8vo. bds. 5s.

This edition of the Apology supplies what has long been considered desirable—a series of explanatory and historical Notes and an Index.

JUSTIN MARTYR.

1.

S. Justini Philosophi et Martyris Apologia Prima.

Edited, with a corrected Text and English Introduction, containing a Life of the Author and explanatory Notes, by the Rev. W. Trollope, M.A., Pembroke College, Cambridge. 8vo. bds. 7s. 6d.

2.

Justin Martyr's Dialogue with Trypho the Jew.

Translated from the Greek into the English, with Notes, chiefly for the advantage of English Readers; a Preliminary Dissertation, and a short Analysis. By Henry Brown, M.A. (Originally printed in 1745.) 8vo. bds. 9s.

JUVENAL.

Juvenal: chiefly from the Text of Jahn:

With English Notes for the use of Schools. By J. E. Mayor, M.A., Fellow of St. John's College, Cambridge. *Preparing.*

By the Rev. H. *LATHAM*, M.A.

Fellow and Tutor of Trinity Hall, Cambridge.

Geometrical Problems in the Properties of Conic Sections.

8vo. 3s. 6d.

WILLIAM *LAW*, M.A.;

Edited by Professor *MAURICE.*

Remarks on the Fable of the Bees.

With an Introduction. By the Rev. F. D. Maurice, M.A., Professor of Theology in King's College, London. 12mo. bds. 4s. 6d.

Le Bas Prize Essay.

SCOTT, C. B., for 1849. 8vo. sewed, 2s. 6d.

Subject—"The Greek Kingdoms of Bactria and its vicinity."

Cambridge.

By the Rev. T. *LUND*, B.D.,
late Fellow of St. John's College, Cambridge.

1.

A Short and Easy Course of Algebra.

Chiefly designed for the use of the Junior Classes in Schools, with a numerous collection of Original Easy Exercises. 12mo. bound in cloth, 3*s*. 6*d*. *A new Edition.* *Ready.*

"*His definitions are admirable for their simplicity and clearness.*"
ATHENÆUM.

"*In order to ascertain how far the Author's performance comes up to his design, we have paid particular attention to those places where the learner is most likely to stumble upon acknowledged difficulties. . . . In all these we have much reason to admire the happy art of the Author in making crooked things straight, and rough places smooth. The Student must be hopelessly obtuse who does not, in following the guidance of Mr. Lund, obtain increasing light and satisfaction in every step of his way; and such, too, is the strictly scientific as well as simple nature of the course pursued, that he who makes himself master of it, will have laid a firm foundation for an extensive and lofty superstructure of mathematical acquirement.*"
THE EDUCATOR.

"*Admirably planned. . . . very successful.*"—THE WELSHMAN.

2.

Wood's Elements of Algebra.

Designed for the use of Students in the Universities. Carefully Revised and enlarged with Notes, additional Propositions, and Examples. Thirteenth Edition. 8vo. bds. 12s. 6d.

3.

A Companion to Wood's Algebra.

Containing Solutions of various Questions and Problems in Algebra, and forming a Key to the chief difficulties found in the Collection of Examples appended to Wood's Algebra. Twelfth Edition. 8vo. sewed, 6s.

By HENRY *MACKENZIE*, B.A.,
Scholar of Trinity College, Cambridge.

"The Beneficial Influence of the Christian Clergy during the
first thousand years of the Christian Era," being the Essay which obtained the Hulsean Prize for 1850. *In Preparation.*

By Professor *M'COY.*

Description of British Palaeozoic Fossils,
Added by Professor Sedgwick to the Woodwardian Collection, and contained in the Geological Museum of the University of Cambridge.

Fasciculus I., containing the Radiata and Articulata. With 11 Plates. 4to. sewed, 16s.

Fasciculus II., containing the Mollusca and Vertebrata.
In the Press.

By R. *MOON,* M.A.,
Fellow of Queens' College, Cambridge.

1.

Fresnel and his Followers. A Criticism.
To which are appended Outlines of Theories of Diffraction and Transversal Vibration. 8vo. bds. 5s.

2.

A Reply to the Calumnies of the 'Athenæum.'
8vo. sewed, 1s.

3.

Professor Challis and Professor Tardy.
The New Equation in Hydrodynamics. 8vo. sewed, 1s.

SOAMES' MOSHEIM.

Mosheim's Institutes of Ecclesiastical History, Ancient and Modern. A New Translation, by D. Murdock. Edited, with additions, by Henry Soames, M.A. 4 vols. 8vo. cloth, £2 8s.

"*Mr. Soames has added to this edition, matter amounting to about one volume, chiefly connected with the English Church, on which subject Mosheim's otherwise admirable work is considered deficient.*"

By the Rev. W. *NIND,* M.A.,
Fellow of St. Peter's College, Cambridge.

Klopstock's Odes.
Translated from the German. Fcap. 8vo. cloth, 6s.

Edited by the Rev. J. P. *NORRIS,* M.A.,
Fellow of Trinity College, Cambridge, and one of Her Majesty's Inspectors of Schools.

Ten School-Room Addresses. 18mo. sewed, 8d.

Cambridge.

Norrisian Prize-Essays.

JONES, J. H., for 1846. 8vo. sewed, 2s. 6d.
Subject—"If they hear not Moses and the Prophets, neither will they be persuaded if one rose from the dead."

KINGSBURY, T. L., for 1847. 8vo. sewed, 3s. 6d.
Subject—"On the Connexion between the Prophetic and the other Evidences of Christianity."

WHITTINGTON, R., for 1849. 8vo. bds. 4s. 6d.
Subject—"The internal Evidence afforded by the Historical Books of the Old Testament, that the several Writers of them were inspired by the Holy Ghost."

HUGH JAMES *ROSE'S* PARKHURST.

Parkhurst's Greek and English Lexicon to the New Testament,

with Additions, by HUGH JAMES ROSE, revised by J. R. MAJOR. A New Edition. 8vo. cloth, £1 1s.

"MR. ROSE HAS ADDED AT LEAST ONE-THIRD OF NEW MATTER TO THIS WORK."—*Horne.*

"*This is now admitted to be the best Lexicon to the Greek Testament. The Examples are so numerous as to give it almost all the advantages of a Concordance: and its explanations may often save reference to a Commentary.*"

By J. B. *PHEAR*, M.A.,
Fellow and Mathematical Lecturer of Clare Hall, Cambridge.

Elementary Mechanics,

Accompanied by numerous Examples solved Geometrically. 8vo. bds. 10s. 6d.

PLATO.

1.

Plato's Republic:

A new Translation into English, with an Introduction and Notes. By TWO FELLOWS of Trin. Coll., Cambridge. *In Preparation.*

2.

Plato's Republic, Book I.

Translated by the Rev. A. R. GRANT, M.A., Fellow and Assistant Tutor of Trinity College. 12mo. sewed, 1s. 6d.

POPE.

The Works of Alexander Pope, including his Letters.

With a new Life of the Author and Notes on the Poems, by WILLIAM ROSCOE. 8 vols. 8vo. cloth, (best trade Edition,) £4 4s.

By the Rev. J. H. *PRATT*, M.A.,
Fellow of Caius College, Cambridge.

The Mathematical Principles of Mechanical Philosophy, and

their Applications to Elementary Mechanics and Architecture, but chiefly to the Theory of Universal Gravitation. Second Edition, revised and improved. 8vo. bds. £1 1s.

Cambridge.

Bp. JEREMY *TAYLOR*:
Edited by the Rev. Charles Page Eden, M.A., Fellow of Oriel College, Oxford.

Complete Works:
With Life by Bp. Heber. A new Edition, with the References carefully verified, and a copious Index. To be completed in 10 vols. 8vo. cloth, 10s. 6d. each.

Vols. II. to IX. are already published.

Vol. 2, Life of Christ.—Vol. 3, Holy Living and Dying.—Vol. 4, Sermons for all Sundays in the Year.—Vol. 5, Episcopacy, &c., and Minor Works.—Vol. 6, Real Presence of Christ, &c.—Vol. 7, Repentance, Golden Grove, &c.—Vol. 8, Treatises against Popery.—Vol. 9, Ductor Dubitantium.

By the Rev. E. *THRING*, M.A.,
Fellow of King's College, Cambridge.

The Elements of Grammar taught in English.
18mo. bound in cloth, 2s.

"*A very able book it is, both in substance and form.*"—Spectator.

"*We have no hesitation in saying that this is one of the cleverest and happiest productions. The advantage of this* vade mecum *is that the cold skeleton of the driest subject in the world is clothed with plumpness and positive attraction.......It is in truth a most refreshing and admirable work*—a genuine contribution to the wants of the age."—Christian Times.

"*A clever and scientific little book.*"—Guardian.

By the Rev. J. H. *TITCOMB.*

Bible Studies, or an Inquiry into the Progressive Development of Divine Revelation. Part I. 8vo. cloth, 3s. 6d.

By I. *TODHUNTER*, M.A.,
Fellow of St. John's College, Cambridge.

An Elementary Treatise on the Differential Calculus.
About Christmas.

This Work is intended for the use of Schools as well as for Students in the Universities.

By the Rev. RICHARD CHENEVIX *TRENCH*, M.A.,
of Trinity College, Cambridge, Professor of Theology in King's College, London, and Author of "Notes on the Parables."

The Fitness of Holy Scripture for Unfolding the Spiritual Life of Man: Christ the Desire of all Nations; or the Unconscious Prophecies of Heathendom. Being the Hulsean Lectures for the years 1845 and 1846. Second Edition. 8vo. bds. 7s. 6d.

By the Rev. JOHN *WARREN*,
late Fellow and Tutor of Jesus College, Cambridge.

A Treatise on the Geometrical Representation of the Square Root of Negative Quantities. 8vo. bds. 5s.

By W. P. *WILSON*, M.A.,
Fellow of St. John's College, Cambridge, and Professor of Mathematics in Queen's College, Belfast.

A Treatise on Dynamics. 8vo. bds. 9s. 6d.

By the Rev. Dr. *WOOD*,
late Master of St. John's College, Cambridge.

The Elements of Algebra.
Designed for the use of Students in the University. Thirteenth Edition, carefully revised and enlarged, with Notes, additional Propositions and Examples. By THOMAS LUND, B.D. 8vo. bds. 12s. 6d.

By J. *WRIGHT*, M.A.,
of Trinity College, Cambridge, and Head-Master of Sutton Coldfield Grammar School.

The History of Greece in Greek,
From the Invasion of Xerxes to the Peloponnesian War: as related by Diodorus and Thucydides, with Explanatory Notes, Critical and Historical, for the use of Schools. *Preparing.*

XENOPHON.

Memorabilia, Book IV.
Literally translated into English Prose, with a brief Memoir of Socrates, and Notes. By EDWARD BRINE, B.A., Scholar of Queens' College, Cambridge. 12mo. sewed, 2s. 6d.

By the Rev. BROOKE FOSS *WESTCOTT*, M.A.,
Fellow of Trinity College, Cambridge.

1.

The Elements of the Gospel Harmony;
With a Catena on INSPIRATION, from the Writings of the Ante-Nicene Fathers. Crown 8vo. cloth, 6s. 6d.

"*The production of a young Theologian of great promise.*"
T. K. ARNOLD.

"*The most remarkable and original part of the work is a long and most carefully executed exposition of the Ante-Nicene Doctrine of Inspiration, drawn directly from the writings of the Fathers themselves: and a very interesting account of some of the heretical Gospels and the little-known Clementines.*"—THE GUARDIAN.

"*The Author argues very ably for the plenary inspiration of the Gospels. . . . . A large amount of learning is brought to bear on the subject.*"—ENGLISH REVIEW.

"*Admirably conceived, arranged, and expressed.*"
FREE CHURCH MAGAZINE.

2.

The Elements of Apostolic Harmony;
An attempt to determine the separate purposes and mutual relations of the Canonical Epistles. *Preparing.*

www.ingramcontent.com/pod-product-compliance
Lightning Source LLC
LaVergne TN
LVHW021412110826
845150LV00007B/1895